Successor journal to *Theatre Q*
VOLUME XIV   NUMBE

NEW
THEATRE
QUARTERLY

Editors
CLIVE BARKER
SIMON TRUSSLER

Advisory Editors: Arthur Ballet, Eugenio Barba, Susan Bassnett,
Tracy Davis, Martin Esslin, Maggie Gale (*Book Reviews Editor*),
Lizbeth Goodman, Peter Hepple, Ian Herbert, Jan Kott,
Brian Murphy, Sarah Stanton, Ian Watson

Contents

*New Theatre Quarterly is published in February, May, August, and November by Cambridge University Press, The Edinburgh
Building, Shaftesbury Road, Cambridge CB2 2RU, England*   ISBN 0 521 62690 0   ISSN 0266 – 464X

Editorial Enquiries

Great Robhurst, Woodchurch, Ashford, Kent TN26 3TB, England

Unsolicited manuscripts are considered for publication in *New Theatre Quarterly*. They should be sent to Simon Trussler at the above address, but unless accompanied by a stamped addressed envelope (UK stamp or international reply coupons) return cannot be guaranteed. Contributors are asked to follow the journal's house style as closely as possible.

Subscriptions

New Theatre Quarterly (ISSN: 0266-464X) is published quarterly by Cambridge University Press, The Edinburgh Building, Shaftesbury Road, Cambridge CB2 2RU, UK, and The Journals Department, 40 West 20th Street, New York, NY 10011-4211, USA.

Four parts form a volume. The subscription price, which includes postage (excluding VAT), of Volume XIV, 1998, is £49.00 (US$85.00 in the USA, Canada and Mexico) for institutions, £28.00 (US$44.00) for individuals ordering direct from the publishers and certifying that the Journal is for their personal use. Single parts cost £13.00 (US$23.00 in the USA, Canada and Mexico) plus postage. EU subscribers (outside the UK) who are not registered for VAT should add VAT at their country's rate. VAT registered subscribers should provide their VAT registration number. Prices include delivery by air. Japanese prices for institutions are available from Kinokuniya Company Ltd., P.O. Box 55, Chitose, Tokyo 156, Japan.

Orders, which must be accompanied by payment, may be sent to a bookseller or to the publishers (in the USA, Canada and Mexico to the North American Branch). Periodicals postage paid at New York, NY, and at additional mailing offices. POSTMASTER: send address changes in the USA, Canada and Mexico to *New Theatre Quarterly*, Cambridge University Press, The Journals Department, 40 West 20th Street, New York, NY 10011-4211.

Claims for missing issues will only be considered if made immediately on receipt of the following issue.

Information on *New Theatre Quarterly* and all other Cambridge journals can be accessed via http://www.cup.cam.ac.uk/ and in North America via http://www.cup.org/.

The Edinburgh Building, Cambridge CB2 2RU, United Kingdom
40 West 20th Street, New York, NY 10011-4211, USA
10 Stamford Road, Oakleigh, Melbourne 3166, Australia

Typeset by Country Setting, Woodchurch, Ashford, Kent TN26 3TB
Printed and bound in the United Kingdom at the University Press, Cambridge

Charles Marowitz

Otherness: the Director and the Discovery of the Actor

Charles Marowitz worked extensively as a director in Britain from the late 'fifties through the 'seventies, and was one of the editors of the influential *Encore* magazine in the formative years of the 'new wave'. His free-lance work included the co-direction with Peter Brook of the seminal 'Theatre of Cruelty' season, and the premiere production of Joe Orton's *Loot*. Later, in partnership with Jim Haynes, a season at the London Traverse Theatre led to the creation of his own, more enduring Open Space Theatre in a basement in Tottenham Court Road – one of the identifying events of 1968 and its theatrical aftermath. Since returning to his native United States, Marowitz has worked out of Malibu, and continued his parallel role as writer – in which he has become best known for his sequence of 'collage' Shakespeares ranging from *Hamlet* to *The Shrew*, and also as a self-professed 'counterfeit critic' and theoretician of acting and directing. The following article also forms the final chapter of his latest book, *The Other Way: an Alternative Approach to Acting and Directing*, to be published by Applause Books later this year. It represents, also, a concise charting of his own voyage of discovery – of the role of the director, and of the recognition of the autonomy and 'higher calling' of the actor that this has involved.

WHEN I STARTED in the theatre, I believed a director was the chess-master, the stage the board, and the actors the chess pieces. In my mind, the actors' prime function was to delineate a preconceived pattern of my own making. The hardest thing, I found, was getting them to move about the board – for I realized that every cross, every sit and every rise, was an expression of some intricate inner necessity which either told the story or obfuscated it. I spent a lot of time doodling diagrams on the margins of scripts to ensure that people would execute my choreography.

Most of these preparations were in vain. Invariably my actors' instincts sent them in different directions and inevitably my master-plan would be upset by their maddening unpredictability. Gradually, I abandoned the whole notion of a master plan and came to rehearsals with no prescribed moves at all, armed only with a grasp of what I thought the scene was about. As we worked, I allowed myself to be guided by impulses received during rehearsals – a cross here, a turn there – allowing things

spontaneously to combust. I took this to be a great step forward because, as a director, I had stopped directing *myself* and began instead to find the 'directions' indicated by the actors in the give-and-take of rehearsals.

It is generally agreed that the pattern of movement in a play is the externalization of the way a director visualizes it and, by and large, actors tend to accept the spatial relationships imposed by the director. But after I had relinquished my prerogative to work from a blueprint, I was taking my cue not from my own preconceptions, but from what I took to be the spontaneous impulses of my actors. I was still 'directing' in that I now accepted certain moves and modified others, but in a very crucial sense the fulcrum had shifted.

That, I believed, was the beginning of a certain wisdom, but as time went on I came to realize that the natural impulse of most actors was towards what one might call conditioned social reflexes – rising to greet someone who had come into the room; pacing about to convey anxiety or confusion; slumping into a chair to express

3

contemplation or fatigue. It was not so much that these movements were false but that they signalled emotional responses which had as much to do with ingrained stage custom as with the patterns of human behaviour. It soon occurred to me that contrary motion or contradictory movement could be just as effective, since people often moved in order to compensate for what they were feeling – and what they were feeling was usually very different from what they were saying.

Logistical Support for Self-Discovery

Later I came to understand that behind the realm of psychology there lurked a deeper motivation, one which the characters themselves were often unaware of, and that if you dug deeply enough you could uproot a physical pattern which stood in the same relation to social behaviour as the latent content of dreams did to their manifest content. I came to see that physical movement by and large was a language, like verbal language, which had as many layers as the individual had secrets to hide or emotions to suppress, and that behaviour, far from being motion reflected in a looking-glass, was more like light refracted through a prism.

I started to reverse all my earlier findings. Rather than accept those signal impulses which 'came naturally' to actors and actresses, I delved into what was deeper than their apparent 'natures', seeking that which their 'natures' were avoiding or denying. This meant that as I could not accept my own first instincts in regard to the geography of the scene, so I could not accept those of the actors either. We all had to go further than our first instincts – into areas which were as clouded for them as they were for myself.

But a director, not being an actor, has not conditioned his body to ferret out and then express what is most deeply embedded in his psyche. He may divine it or probe it intellectually, but only the actor can find it kinetically and bring it to the surface. The director's job, I came to realize, was to provide the logistical support needed by the actor to make those self-discoveries, and to reject the practised impulses that frequently blocked the way towards unearthing what lay deeper.

It appeared that inside every actor there was a hidden actor. Although occasionally glimpsed behind language or characterization, he or she never wholly surfaced, but often had 'moments' or 'flashes' where certain remarkable things were glimpsed. Through exercises that transcended his normal social functioning, the hidden actor could occasionally be revealed and, when he was, his uniqueness stood in striking contrast to the more conventional personage that normally negotiated on his behalf. He was much freer and uninhibited than his surface self and in much closer contact with his deeper instincts.

More essence than matter, he could none the less shape matter so that it became essential. Although intrinsically abstract, he was constantly looking for ways to make his abstractness concrete. When given free reign he could transform his characters, investing them with the uniqueness of his own being. The shell of studied characteristics would split apart to reveal a fascinating human being unlike anyone else. When that hidden nature coalesced with inspiration, it brought inert material to life, and the hidden actor now revealed astonished everyone with whom he came into contact.

How to reach that hidden actor and marshal his resources became the object of intensive labour – and it was a task made more strenuous by the fact that no formula existed by which he could be rooted out. It was as hit-and-miss as everything else that took place in the rehearsal situation, the difference being that one knew that what one was searching for could never be found in the superficies of rehearsal and that everything in the production procedure militated against its discovery.

It was in the resourcefulness and inventiveness of the hidden actor that the surface actor could break through and install the best part of himself on stage, but ironically it was the timidities and anxieties of the surface actor that created the barrier which obstructed his emergence. The prime object of rehearsals, then, was to create the conditions through which the surface actor could be usurped and the hidden actor installed: and the way to bring this about depended on a delicate conjunction between director and performer. The certainty that this 'other actor' was there justified all the anguish and frustration involved in working with his superficial counterpart.

The Inner Structure of Character

Insights about acting chemistry threw the written word into a different perspective. Text – yes. And behind that – sub-text. But what was behind *that*? Character, yes, but from what stage in a person's life? Their adolescence, their childhood, their infancy? If the child lives on in the adult, what portion of the adult is made up of the child? What cloaking modifications have been devised by the adult? At what point in the civilizing process does the savage get entirely eliminated, leaving only the socially adjusted individual? If a successful and effective black general, fiendishly manipulated into vengeance and jealousy, can turn into something primitive and murderous, does that mean that the upright general was merely a facade? Would the facade have remained intact if the psychological pressures had never been applied?

And what would Hamlet have become, I wonder, if never prodded by the visitation of his ghostly father? Would he simply have adjusted to the new dispensation, married Ophelia, suppressed his regal ambitions, made up with his mother, and settled for a cabinet post – Minister of Education maybe – in the new regime?

All these questions are prompted by the underlying questions: what does the inner structure of a character consist of, and to what extent should these non-manifest possibilities be taken into account in his social persona, given the fact that, under extraordinary circumstances, any one of them can rise to the surface?

By dismantling the director's prerogative to impose moves and actions upon my actors, I had opened a Pandora's box which ultimately put into question everything a director should do in the theatre. If each character's personal motivation was unique unto himself, was it not false and arbitrary to try to unify them according to one man's – the director's – vision? But then, if every character was given free reign, what did that portend for the unity of the whole? Was a disparate and variegated result justifiable on the grounds that it more faithfully reflected the way people actually behaved? But then art, I reminded myself, was not primarily concerned with verisimilitude. The artists – the playwright, director, and acting company – made their own unity in the work of art which paralleled or augmented the reality on which it was ostensibly based.

After countless circumlocutions around the subject, one was back to square one: but the doubts and contradictions would not go away. Clearly, the business of rehearsals was finding things which were not immediately apparent, but if one fell into a formulaic search it became something of a child's treasure hunt – unearthing only what had already been planted in order to be discovered. The first question which demanded to be answered was: what was one looking for? And the next, where in the actor's psyche and the playwright's material did one conduct these searches? The third and most pressing question was: with what tools did one carry out these investigations?

Intellectual analysis was a given – for no sooner did one read a play or examine one's role than the mind began to suggest a number of interpretive possibilities. Improvisation and exercise were two other tools, and with them the actor could 'experience' information which might cast light on hidden areas of the work. Then there was the stimulus to be had from others, the leads provided by fellow actors who, in trying to solve their own problems, threw up provocative challenges to others. To make this tool available, one had to make sure there was an open line of communication to fellow actors which meant reaching out to them without impeding one's own inventions. But in gainfully employing all these tools, there was an initial obstruction which had first to be removed: and that was the most formidable obstacle of all.

Just as the actor had an accretion of tricks, of mannerisms, short cuts, and inculcated clichés, so the director was burdened with prior assumptions, coagulated beliefs, old admirations unconsciously yearning to be duplicated – not to mention a whole storehouse of received wisdom which, once acquired, tended to go unchallenged. The commencement of rehearsals was like the meeting of two magicians, each balancing his own bag of tricks on his back and each assuming his was the largest and most spectacular.

Changing the Starting-Point

Before one ever got to the issues of the play, one had to negotiate the smouldering but tacit demands of each of its participants. This involved wheedling, deviousness, and dollops of child psychology on the part of the director; treachery, elusiveness, and duplicity on the part of the actor. Meanwhile the author stood by watching his work unravel and wondering if, when it was all put together again, it would ever resemble his original creation. Illusions of grandeur and premonitions of disaster hung heavy in the air and, to make matters worse, the tyrannical clock forbade experiment or time spent investigating tantalizing side turnings which, if explored, might yet have yielded marvels which adherence to strict schedules invariably shut off.

Once the starting-point was, so to speak, to change the starting-point, everything else followed from that. The attitude behind the work became defensive – to ward off those conditioned reflexes which, like diseased cells, prevented healthy ones from forming. A new strategy was required to avoid the old pitfalls.

The notion of an ur-text was considered valuable, if only because it held out the promise of life beyond sub-text. Taking an oblique path to the material via improvisation and root exercises was also beneficial in that it widened the parameters of a written work, allowing ideas to enter its airspace from every point of the compass. As soon as one saw a play as part of a greater entity, it gave actors an opportunity to discover more ramifications than could be found in the closed-circuit work of art.

It also reminded artists that a slice of life, no matter what its dimensions, had to be sliced from something greater than itself, and that identifying that larger mass widened the actors' scope and encouraged them to look beyond the parameters set by the playwright. In consequence, the actor was raised to the level of both the playwright and the director, and, released from his traditional subjugation to text and *mise-en-scène*, offered a major role in collaboration rather than the self-effacing role of the dutiful interpreter. Certain floodgates which encouraged egotism and idiosyncrasy to run riot were also opened – but there is never a genuine breakthrough in either art or science that doesn't carry with it the danger of abuse.

What gradually emerged was the realization that the secret at the heart of theatre – if not of all art – was complexity, and that fastening onto one reductive system which seemed to explain and codify it was to evade some much larger issues. Experience was not there to be compressed into a formula, but translated into as many theorems as seemed to pertain to its endless variety.

The quest was not for a system or a method, but for a state of mind which might succeed in capturing the theatre's ever-changing multiplicity. Systematization and methodology fostered the delusion of having cracked the nut, but no one system or methodology could crack every nut. There were more nuts than there were systems to contain them.

In order to achieve the most definitive theatrical result, a technique was needed which was at least as complex as the problem: one that didn't complacently accept the notion that acting was merely projected personality and the theatre the automatic assembly of the playwright's words. It was precisely this kind of niggling dissatisfaction with prevailing standards which had inspired earlier artists to probe more deeply, to reject the familiar and the customary, the manufactured replicas and the reasonable facsimiles. Viewed in a larger perspective, acting theory was essentially a branch of political science, and just as Stanislavsky, Brecht, and Artaud had rejected the reactionary practices of their predecessors, so were we beholden to challenge the implicit social and behavioural customs which ran beneath what we, parcelling them off from larger indivisible things, called acting technique. To be an actor, then, meant being a critic of both art and life: and for the effective actor the criticism had then to be converted into practical manoeuvres which combated the banalities of art in order to avoid reproducing the clichés of life.

Actor as Force-Field

Ploddingly, through a series of stumbles and detours, collisions with stone walls, and wanderings up blind alleys, I came to realize that the actor doesn't so much 'build a character' as step into a magnetic field where he is affected by emanations from the ideas, impulses, and environment dictated by the production – he doesn't so much 'become a character' or 'live a role' as absorb actions, feelings, and experiences relative to his character and, in so doing, trigger like-actions, like-feelings and like-experiences in his own being; that the actor is a conductor-of-energies *already mobilized* and ready to leap into parallel situations; that he doesn't 'perform' so much as allow the psychic functioning of his character to release universal information already bred in his bone and etched upon his memory; that phylogeny precedes psychology, and that the physical is only the most conspicuous aspect of the metaphysical; that, in fact, the whole notion of constructing a performance – brick by brick, beat by beat, choice by choice – is a bogus linear illusion fostered by over a hundred years of outworn acting theory and inculcated by a mechanistic philosophy which modern science has effectively refuted, although its residue remains lodged in the actors' mind and locked in his musculature; that the actor is not the walking duality described by thinkers as diverse as Gordon Craig, Constantin Stanislavsky, Antonin Artaud, and Bertolt Brecht, but a force-field where memories and habits, originated in pre-history and the primordial slime, dynamically interact, and that every evolutionary development which has refined the human organism over the millennia plays *some* part and exerts *some* influence in the living present; that being an actor is not so much a question of 'training' or 'development' but of awakening susceptibilities to a play's situations, stated and implied, the playwright's intentions, latent and overt, the director's interpretation, articulated and inchoate.

What needed to be abandoned was the idea that an actor was an accretion of conscious manoeuvres such as memorization, blocking, and psychological intent, instead of a catalytic agent which synthesizes all of these things, filtering them through an acting metabolism which enables him to recreate past experience rooted in conscious and pre-conscious memory, and which, under favourable conditions, can manifest itself; that acting was not something you 'do' but something done *to you* if you are free enough to discard clogging formulae and reductive egotism and open yourself up instead to a kind of eternal consciousness of which personal psychology is only the tip of the iceberg.

Having diverged so far from what was considered practical and customary, I was then struck with the chastening realization that if one recoiled from abstractions such as these and took refuge in nuts-and-bolts, in 'units and objectives', in provable premises and common practices, one was cosying oneself into an hermetically-sealed capsule which, though it looked like the macrocosm, was actually a microcosm.

The theatre is a serial art. Actors and directors go from play to play often working in very different circumstances and also on highly contrasting material. Unless blessed with the continuity of working in a permanent ensemble in its own venue, each production represents a new start. The insights and refinements created with a previous group of actors do not automatically transfer to a new company. One has to begin all over again, and the tendency to do so tends to mechanize a process which should be ongoing and regenerative.

A Sense of a Higher Calling

Many of the problems thrown up by work in the theatre would either be solved or considerably reduced if the same director worked with the same actors over an extended period of time. After a while, a group intelligence is engendered which becomes greater than the director's and the actors' intelligence combined. But so long as the theatre remains an *ad hoc* art form, it will be necessary to formulate a *modus operandi* to enable it to start afresh each time.

The key, in my view, is constantly to maintain a kind of flexible scepticism – a deep-seated reluctance to accept what comes too easily (often automatically) and then construe it as being 'natural'. What comes most 'naturally' to both actors and directors is the tendency to repeat themselves – to print out what has been pre-programmed.

Whenever a company of actors assemble, the onus is always the same: they must for the sake of the work before them form an ensemble, provide a gloss peculiar to themselves and their work situation, realize a joint conception of the work in conjunction with the other members of the artistic team, and resolve not to repeat what has been done before or promote novelty for its own sake.

Because the theatre has to a large extent become routine, play production has become standardized. No sooner do rehearsals begin than artists feel the pressure to deliver results. Because the text is the most tangible element in the process, it is clung onto for dear life. Language is memorized, organized, physically circumscribed – and, before the most elementary secrets of the play are explored or discovered, coagulated. During this process there are gestures to characterization, allusions to sub-text, and lip-service to thematic ideas, but the object of the journey is to arrive at one's destination as promptly as possible. The landscape is

never glimpsed and, like suburbanites having dutifully caught the 7.04, the commuters conceal themselves behind newspapers so as to have only the most minimal contact with their fellow-passengers. And when the train finally pulls in to the station, everyone goes their own way.

But the actor's journey must be the antithesis of the commuter's. There should be dialogue, discussion, and the vigorous interchange of ideas all along the way. Every bit of landscape needs to be assimilated; every passing observation analyzed and disputed. On arrival, everyone should jam into the same taxi and be driven to the same address. The arrival should be thought of as the springboard for a new departure; the performance not the pay-off of rehearsals, but the first phase of the grander journey which is the run of the play.

What hampers us are age-old obstacles: complacency, habitude, ego, and the irresistible tug of the familiar. The economics of the theatre promote the idea that an actor is a unit-of-labour purchased at the lowest possible cost and then inserted into a larger mechanism which, like him or herself, has limited usefulness and is easily replaceable. But the transient nature of the actor's art is belied by the fact that it has been extant for countless centuries, and, although generations come and go, varieties of perception contained in timeless artifacts survive in a world without end.

That sense of being part of something vast and endlessly renewing is what should give the actor a sense of a higher calling which no amount of professional indignity can demean. The actor who feels he is being 'slotted into a role' will act accordingly. The actor who believes that he is being summoned to perform a task which has also exercised the keenest sensibilities of both antiquity and modern times will recognize that only the most strenuous personal effort will qualify him to take his place in the history of the art to which he aspires.

We're all lying in the gutter, said Wilde, but some of us are looking at the stars. The angle of one's head makes all the difference.

John Russell Brown

Theatrical Pillage in Asia: Redirecting the Intercultural Traffic

The potential and the problems of multicultural theatre have frequently been described and debated in this as in other theatre journals, but discussions of its value and viability have generally been in ethical terms – over how far it is possible for the West to 'import' or otherwise employ the theatrical traditions of other cultures without resort to an imperialist appropriation of what is found 'consumable', to the detriment of the culture thus despoiled. While not ignoring the moral arguments, John Russell Brown here deals also with the practical issues – notably, how far different kinds of theatre depend on being 'site-specific' not only in terms of the performers involved, but also in terms of audiences and their responses. He argues that, paradoxically, truly intercultural theatre is more often to be found where western influences from Hollywood films or pop music have become part of the lived experience of eastern cultures, or in western communities where (for example) British and West Indian or 'Anglo' and Latino-American traditions have become intertwined. He suggests that rather than trying to embrace the substance of 'other' traditions, western theatre might better benefit by exploring the conventions that modulate the relationship between actors and audience, or the approach of the actor to different kinds of 'text'. He concludes: 'By using overseas research to develop its own inheritance, a theatre might discover what it alone needs to create and encourage a more active and imaginative response from its local audience.' A widely published writer on drama and theatre, John Russell Brown was first Head of the University of Birmingham's Department of Drama and Theatre Arts, and was subsequently an Associate Director at the National Theatre in London. Currently he is visiting Professor at Columbia University, New York.

ARIANE MNOUCHKINE and Peter Brook are the most accomplished among the many theatre directors who have visited Asia and returned home to Europe or North America and put what they have found into practice in their own productions.[1] Like raiders across a frontier, they bring back strange clothes as their loot and try to wear them as if to the manner born. Costumes, make-up, masks, music, dances, staging techniques, and (sometimes) texts are all carried off in this way.

Mnouchkine found in Asia 'such beauty in things, in gestures, [and] a simple ceremonial quality', all of which seemed 'indispensable' for the work of her theatre company. 'My love for Asia and for Asian theatre', she was to say, 'has determined much of my work.'[2] So, time and again, Peter Brook was amazed by what he found: in the gaze of performers in a Bengal village,

for example, he saw 'an incredible strength, an unbelieveable intensity', and immediately asked how this was achieved.[3]

Such directors take pride in an enhancement of their work by borrowings from Asian theatres, even though their audiences may be as much mystified as enlightened by the mis-matches of inspiration in the resulting productions, and even though assumed behaviour and appearance may sit awkwardly on actors who have been nurtured in far different circumstances from those who have spent lifetimes in acquiring them.

Theatres in the more financially secure countries of Asia are well aware of the advantages of intercultural traffic. In new buildings modelled on those found in Europe and North America, directors have assumed control over performance in 'western-style' productions, and have borrowed many techniques of staging as a matter of course. In Japan, Ninagawa Yukio uses European music and classic playtexts, adapts the methods of western stage design (although keeping Asian motifs and references), and works with some borrowed rehearsal techniques.

Playtexts (when translated) and music (when recorded) are especially easy to transport and assimilate. Suzuki Tadashi, who centres his work firmly (even aggressively) in ancient Japanese acting techniques and has built himself a traditional style of theatre, none the less uses European music and playtexts – which he then rewrites, rearranges, cuts, and supplements to serve his own purposes.

In many parts of the world, an international theatrical export trade was established long ago. The specially staged and rearranged performances of Balinese dance-dramas and the solo performances by the Beijing Opera star Mei Lanfang are the most notorious examples from the early decades of the twentieth century. Antonin Artaud (and through him many other French intellectuals of the inter-war years) thought that ancient Balinese theatre pointed the way towards the rejuvenation of all theatre. Meyerhold, Eisenstein, and Brecht were similarly inspired by the 'new' ancient Chinese performance art. About the same time, the translator Arthur Waley and the poet W. B. Yeats made some aspects of No theatre accessible in England and Ireland.

In Japan, with the wealth to take the initiative, international borrowing has been taken much further. While keeping to its ancient style as closely as possible, No theatre has gained a new economic prosperity by building a theatre especially for shows that are given at convenient times for tourists, in the middle of days of sightseeing and shopping, and also by supplying lectures, leaflets, short demonstrations, and tourist knick-knacks.

Both national and foreign visitors buy extremely expensive tickets for these performances. They also attend productions of Kabuki and Bunraku, more eye-catching forms of performance that are now housed in huge 'western-style' theatres and staged with some of the technical and directorial devices appropriate to those buildings. Sending the companies on foreign tours promotes knowledge of their different traditions and, on one occasion, examples of all three have been given within a single evening's entertainment.[4]

Perhaps such cultural exchanges flourish in Japan because its ancient theatres have always had to adapt to changing conditions, as commanded by successive shoguns or noblemen, or in response to large, popular, and fee-paying audiences. Ancient Indian theatres, dependent on the life and rituals of temples and not charging for admission, may not be so susceptible to intercultural development and commercial exploitation.

Many extraordinary performances have derived from these cultural 'exchanges' and, as the trade has become common, its repercussions have become widespread and influential. It is time to ask what is being achieved, for the future well-being of both exporters and importers, explorers and explored, exploiters and exploited.

Attracting the Wrong Audiences?

In Europe and North America, imports of staging, costumes, music, and acting techniques can attract audiences among confirmed theatre enthusiasts who make a point of seeking out the latest innovations in theatre and other arts. But this activity is expensive and practicable only for well-subsidized and well-publicized companies that can afford long months of preparation and tour their shows around to seek out specialist audiences. The formula works for the few but does little to help those companies that cannot tour. It does not address the interests of the audiences a building-based company fails at present to attract – and from whom it might discover its own new themes, stories, and characters.

What could be the advantages of experiment with exotic devices when so much unexplored opportunity lies ready at hand? Topical and local icons are everywhere available for use and at less expense than those sought out from distant countries. Conventional gestures and actions found in local and modern life, together with stories that arise from the present time and place or make unmistakable reference to those realities, are all capable of theatrical exploitation, and so are common slogans and a choice of everyday clothes. Theatre performances using home-grown material could speak more directly to their audience's own lives and interests than the time-consuming implants favoured by so many forward-looking directors – at best a very circuitous and difficult route towards satisfying local demands.

The forms favoured for export to Europe and North America in the name of intercultural theatre are usually those of the most ancient and site-specific Asian traditions, and the performances copied have been developed over centuries to serve religious beliefs in which present-day exploiters have no shred of faith, and to reflect lives that in their daily observances and habits are as much unlike those in the industrial West as may be imagined.

In content and techniques of performance, such theatre has little that can reflect a world in which very new technology is rapidly introducing huge changes in lifestyles and ways of thought and feeling. How can turning to ancient and 'foreign' sources help theatre to become the means for viewing in clearer focus those new, irreversible, and impersonal forces for change that are being experienced throughout western society?

Processing Tradition for the Tourist

In Asia, to view the other side of cultural exchange, a growing dependence on sales to the tourist and export trade threatens the well-being of traditional theatres and the maintenance of their own audiences. The explorers from Europe and North America leave wreckage behind them as they spread knowledge of ancient theatres among journalists and tour promoters and show its practitioners what will interest foreign visitors.

To sit among rows of tourists at the Ubud Palace in Bali and watch one of the nightly and routine performances of a 'dance-drama' is to realize how far the exploitation of an indigenous theatre for a western audience can damage its traditions without bringing noticeable advantages. Ill-disciplined and sometimes incompetent teenagers and children will support two or three experienced dancers. Dialogue will be spoken from offstage through amplifiers and attention held by blazing electric lights as the video recorders of visiting professors work continuously from the front row of seats. Balinese performance is changing rapidly, not because of its own needs, but to please a passing trade from other cultures by whatever means will make money.

In Kerala in southernmost India, excerpts of Kathakali and, more recently, of Theyam performances have been especially prepared as portable shows that can be viewed in tourist hotels or taken on visits to specialist audiences in other countries around the world. Removed from their original sites of performance, as defined by location, language, moral and political thought, religion, and other essential elements of lived experience, the costumes' visual splendour and the drama's music and histrionic craft are sufficient to deserve attention and bring back foreign currency that will sustain further work and, at the same time, modify the concepts and processes of performance.

The word Theyam derives from *deivam*, meaning 'pertaining to God': thus, its performance should take place in a holy place and occupy an entire night, passing from representation into trance and divination. Specialist training takes many years and, in its own environment, fasting for several days precedes each performance. Spectators are required to take a journey out of their usual living space to experience each yearly and necessarily unique enactment.

Similarly, Kathakali and the older Kutiyattam were developed to be performed in the presence of the gods within a temple, and should take days or weeks to enact: a short selection of accessible fragments makes very different demands on performers and audiences. By modifying performances to take advantage of cultural trade, those who practice these arts are themselves being changed, as will happen to anyone who turns from giving freely over the course of a lifetime to selling comparatively small and perishable favours.[5]

Exchange cannot work equitably in two directions between two very different societies and theatres: West and East, modern and ancient, economically advantaged and disadvantaged. Costs are heavy in terms of artistic inheritance and an ability to serve any local audience a theatre might attract. At best, it may be called borrowing, but often it would be better described as pillage by force of superior finance and organization. The theatre from which these items have been imitated will be left irrecoverably altered – not least in the attitudes of mind of those who work in them.

Site-Specific Actors – and Audiences

Some aspects of theatre work are very easily influenced and comparatively simple to borrow and imitate. Words, music, stage sets, costumes, and technical equipment can be transported in any direction, East or West. With some little trouble and money, they can be almost faultlessly copied. But the ways in which these elements of theatre are used will not be imitated so easily; to copy a mode of performance rather than the adjuncts of it requires involvement with far less tractable elements.

The fact is that staging devices, words, and music are not at the very heart of any theatre and do not define its nature. Without imitation at the more basic level which depends upon the actors and audience, the accoutrements and setting for performance or the words of a text will not be put to the same use as in their original homes and will not have comparable effect.

The two essential components of theatre have always been the live actors[6] and live audiences. Neither can be exported or become the subject of exchange arrangements since these elements are site-specific and have to be seen in relation to each other at the moment of performance. Being present at a performance before its own audience is the only satisfactory way to begin to appreciate the essence of any remote theatre, and it is this experience which encourages theatre directors to attempt the export of the more accessible features of what they have seen.

No one could pretend that audiences are available for borrowing or imitation, being firmly rooted in time and place. Moreover, they are not very susceptible to change or outside influence, or even to enquiry. A wish to become at one with a 'foreign' audience presents intractable problems, in their own way as impossible as those of transporting hundreds of people from one country to another, from one town to another, or to a rural area or across language borders. Only in very small and very imperfect ways can travellers infiltrate and become part of an audience of which they are not natural members by reason of their lives and their culture.

Richard Schechner pursued the problem of how to respond suitably as an audience member to Indian theatres about as far as any non-Indian could, when he converted to the Hindu religion and received the name of Jayaganesh. Yet this was no more than a pretence, as he subsequently confessed:

As I, a 58-year-old man, write these words, I wonder at the secret spectacle of my Keralan incarnation: a New York man of 42, dressed Indian-style, fretting as only an atheist Jew can over his hypocritical conversion, moving through a crowded temple courtyard – what was this Jayaganesh doing if not performing himself performing his Hinduism?[7]

In some societies more is possible, given sufficient time and talent to penetrate the barriers and become at one with a new audience. Some Japanese specialists – such as the scholar, critic, and playwright Takahashi Yasunari – who have lived for years as students in England, and return there almost annually, can write with authority on theatre experiences in both London and Tokyo. Many Indians from the generations which grew up speaking English have become almost completely at home as audience members in two very different continents.

Yet such individuals do not make up any actual audience, which for ancient and traditional theatres will always be stubbornly their own audiences, belonging to a very local cultural environment. Tourists and foreign students, no matter how well intentioned and informed, can never be more than transient observers of these theatres: still less can they carry this part of a performance back to their homes as loot.

Of the two essential elements of theatre, acting seems rather more copiable than audiences. Actors, anywhere, have much the same physical bodies which are capable of very similar actions and reactions. Exercises and prolonged training can be undertaken whereby one actor can learn to do the same physical movements and make the same sounds as another. The same costumes and make-up can be worn; to some extent, the same dramas can be enacted and rehearsed by similar methods. But all this is not enough to make any two actors alike as performers. Each individual physique and each mental and emotional constitution are in the final analysis unrepeatable; and still less imitable is the mysterious source of an actor's inspiration – what is usually called talent.

Problems of Authenticity

The heart of acting lies in the imagination, and that is rooted in each actor's unique and ineradicable relationship to the society and family in which he or she grew up. These are the sources drawn upon at the further reaches of an actor's art, when the drama demands absolute truth and total presence on stage: these are, finally, what distinguish one actor from another and explain why actors, like audiences, are not available for imitation in an open market of cultural exchange.

An attempt to 'barter'[8] performers with one another, transplanting them from their own social and cultural environments, will not be a true or complete exchange, but an expensive exploitation of the actors who have been dislocated – especially those taken from economically weaker but traditionally stronger societies.

Even between countries that are close enough in culture to share much the same language and economic status, formidable barriers exist between their actors. A person who grew up in North America but studied in a London acting school during his or her formative years will rarely become an English actor without differences being apparent in every challenging role; and, back in the United States, he or she will be recognizable, for some years at least, as an 'English-trained American actor'. Such barriers will be experienced *within* a single country as various as India: only a little experience is needed to recognize when an art such as Kathakali has been studied and learnt for some special production rather than being the style that the performers have learnt since early childhood and used all their professional lives.

Unless a performance has the appropriate inner necessity, which derives from a lifetime's experience inside and outside a theatre, an assumption of all its outer accoutrements – the costumes, make-up, music, postures, gestures, stage behaviour, speech – are only very complicated contrivances that prevent total and instinctive performances and intrude upon the relationship between audience and actors.

This point is illustrated by Christel Weiler's account of the visible differences between the Asian and the American cast members in the No sequences of Robert Wilson's *Knee Plays*. Those who had learnt the Japanese techniques for the production could have had no experience of their sources in lived experience, and so to the viewer there was always a distinctive and alien 'cultural imprint in the actors' bodies'. The Asian performers, in contrast, 'gave the impression of harmony with the patterns of movement. There was no "foreign" nuance in their movement'.[9] And falsity can register mentally as well as physically: in response to the production of *L'Indiade* (1987), Patrice Pavis wrote that 'Mnouchkine's actors . . . appear all the more inauthentic as they attempt to behave like Indians; they speak, think, and dream like products of western humanism'.[10]

Exchange, borrowing, trade, or looting across major frontiers diminishes any theatre because it transgresses its inherited reliance on the society from which the drama takes its life and for which it was intended to be performed. The degree to which a style of performance departs from lived experience is not an important factor in this equation, since both actors and audience members are what they are regardless of any theatrical considerations. However worthily it is intentioned, intercultural theatrical exchange is, in fact, a form of pillage, and the result is fancy-dress pretence or, at best, the creation of a small zoo in which no creature has its full life.

The True Mingling of Traditions

The most thoroughly integrated intercultural theatre will be found in productions which are created within a multicultural society where audience and actors have already been conditioned by imports that other processes have brought into their everyday lives. A prime example is the Jatra (or touring) theatre of Bengal and Orissa in India: in these days, its traditional performances are interrupted or extensively embellished with songs and dances taken directly from cinema and pop music: and these are clearly of the present time, and of Hollywood and European origin.

Old conventions of performance are thus modified as orchestras are augmented with western instruments and as variable lighting and sound amplification are boldly and openly used. Audiences are encouraged to respond to music and images from popular and yet (strictly speaking) alien entertainments, while demonstrative histrionics and lengthy episodic dramas continue very much as they have for hundreds of years.

Old and new, East and West, co-exist and inter-react freely here. When actresses are introduced against older tradition, male performers may still be used for the more powerfully dramatic or comically extrava-

gant female roles. Because films and pop music, stemming from a very different commercial, social, and intellectual world, are undeniably part of the day-to-day experience of both actors and audiences, they find ready access to a theatre proud and expert in its distinctive and indigenous inheritance – a theatre which in earlier times had been no less ready to accept innovations taken from late nineteenth-century British acting troupes when they were part of everyone's experience at that time and place.

In Europe and America other examples of intercultural theatre with full and lively audiences are plentiful – where they are reactive rather than innovative, the result of a recognition of what is already significant within the society which a particular theatre serves. In Britain, audiences will crowd to see performances that are at one and the same time British and Caribbean in inspiration and technique – but these audiences are drawn chiefly from localities where these traditions already co-exist.[11]

The one-person show of Anna Deveare Smith, *Fires in the Mirror*, first performed in New York in 1992, is a well-known example of similar success: it stages actual inter-racial conflicts in Crown Heights, Brooklyn, by reproducing opposing voices in opposing modes for audiences that have experienced something of the same forces in their own lives. This and many other far larger shows demonstrate how Afro-American theatre can all but integrate two different cultures.

The same is true of the American and Hispanic traditions, or the American and Asiatic, or the twentieth-century American and native American. Such intercultural performances find their audiences in areas where the diverse influences have already been brought together, even though they may be in conflict with each other.

Despite all the difficulties, however, intercultural theatre need not be confined to productions that are reactive to social conditions that already exist, nor need it be dependent on taking advantage of superior resources to copy some superficial elements of theatres that are defenceless against predators from another society. Without trying to possess what is not one's own, much may be accomplished.

In responding to the experience of traditional Asian theatre, an urge to create is often very strong. Performances in an unknown language that reflect a life and thought of which the visitor has little or no comprehension will always be imperfectly followed: and yet, besides giving intense pleasure and intellectual challenge, they may also leave behind a craving to find some answering activity – a gift, if possible, to give back for the extraordinary gift that has been received.

A Surrender to Difference

To be able to do this, the traveller should lay down camera and notebook and willingly surrender to what is offered. In such an encounter, nothing can be calculated or substantiated; to give any part of one's mind to those activitives in pursuit of eye-catching and exotic exports would be to fall short in whatever response is possible by someone from the far side of a cultural divide. Past experience and skills in theatre will be useful, but not in any conscious or predatory way: the task is to remain as open as possible and forget about taking advantage.

In all considerable encounters with other theatres that have maintained their ancient traditions and work in ways unknown in the West, the most potentially usable effect is entirely within the traveller's mind: an increased awareness of what any theatre anywhere might achieve; a clearer recognition that theatre operates within a certain spectrum of possibilities, and that the theatre one knows has occupied only a sector of all this.

After wonder at what has been seen comes a sense of what is missing from usual theatrical experiences at home. Then, more slowly, the possibility of creating some kind of performance that could begin to use this awareness of the rest of the spectrum can take possession of the mind. What seems remote and unapproachable can give rise to a sense of new possibilities for the actors and audiences which the traveller already knows very well. Whereas imperfect imita-

tions of the more detachable elements of traditional Asian theatres can be placedonly in incongruent productions, what has been seen of how their actors work and how their audiences come together and react – the two defining elements of any theatre – can be used as models for experiments anywhere using whatever material and experience lies ready at hand.

When the cultural export is invisible and remains so, when it is an increased awareness of what any theatre may be, cultural exchange will be at its most practical and do least harm. Because theatre in the European tradition uses the same basic means as any other, it should be capable, in its own fashion, of developing its own performances so that they operate in other parts of the spectrum of theatrical possibility than they ordinarily do at present.

Without alerting audiences in the West by providing obvious signs of 'foreign' importations, they might, for example, be kept as well-lit as the actors, and not be banished to a darkened auditorium. Then interaction, in both directions, between stage and auditorium would be encouraged as both sides feel more empowered to influence the occasion. As is customary in many Indian and Chinese theatres, a play could be performed with audience members free to continue their own business as well as their own thoughts, encouraged by the sale of food and drink and the licence to move around from place to place. Then attention to the performance would come and go, and audience members find their own concerns mingling with those of the persons in the play as excitement increases and judgement becomes necessary. The actors would be less in control of spectators but the subsequent loss of intensity might encourage a reponse from the audience that was less subservient to what is presented to them, and more able to take the play into its own concerns, perhaps taking a greater hand in shaping the event.

To what extent could a western audience be made aware of the actors who are performing for them, by addressing dialogue between characters to the audience rather than to the characters who are sharing the action of the play? This is frequently done in Jatra performances and is a characteristic of Marathi plays in Bombay: and the popularity of both these theatres is extraordinary by any standards. Crowded audiences support and spur on the actors, as if they were players in a football team who gain and also respond to the spectators' appreciative enthusiasm. Would this kind of theatre be possible elsewhere if the audience–stage relationship were made more open and so became a major part of the performers' concern? History tells us that this would be the recovery of a lost European tradition.

Points of Possible Contact

Could musicians take their timing from the performers, as they normally do in India and China, and not use a printed score and a conductor as so frequently in European theatres? Such a change would enable music to enhance performance without giving the actors a rigid scheme within which they have to play – and therefore without inhibiting their improvisation. Recorded music with all its prearranged cues could not be used and actors might also have to be musicians, providing their own accompaniment. This would have the further consequence of promoting the audience's sense of the wholeness as well as the immediacy of a play in performance.

Can folk dances and martial arts, as exercised in Japan, China, Korea, and India, or acrobatics, as practised by Chinese actors, suggest ways to gain greater energy in performance by developing certain of the small conventions of daily social intercourse into lively physical statements understood by actors and audiences in common – capable of binding movements together and making oppositions clearer, as these physical skills undoubtedly do in Asia?

The silent attentiveness of the manipulators of puppets in the Japanese Bunraku tradition communicates to an audience and heightens its involvement with the actions of the puppets: does this hold any clues to developing a western audience's reaction to dramatic climaxes? Masks, puppets, extravagant and exotic costumes, cumbersome regalia, ceremonies, dances: all these can be imitated in a parrot-like way, but the more interesting quest would be to seek out ways in which these accountrements alter how theatre is created and what theatre is able to do, and then to ask whether European theatres can take any moves in those directions by using whatever equivalent material is available in their own cultures.

Certain to be more difficult would be the development of acting techniques so refined as those found in No or Kutiyattam, creating individual performances that are as completely realized and so without unwilled or unnecessary activity that they become transparent and offer the audience an imaginative involvement with the actors' imaginations as they become the characters of the drama. What is remarkable here is intensity and sensitivity, the means whereby each moment is open to fresh perception and mutual creativity. Western theatre that tries to show remarkable persons as they are caught up in the drama is far removed in its effect – dependent upon giving strong outward expressions to individual feeling rather than evoking and relying on the audience's imaginative involvement with individual consciousness.

There may, however, be one point of contact here across the cultures. In Europe, a great actor does occasionally appear to be doing almost nothing, and members of the audience, entering into the character's mind, supply what more is needed in terms of their own individual imaginations. At some climaxes in Shakespeare's plays the author seems to have expected this effect, and therefore has provided little by way of text. Examples include the last moments of King Lear as he loses consciousness or of Othello after he has completed his final speech, or of Iago as he silently watches the hero's death and the words spoken by other characters insist that the audience watches him closely. Without the indwelling of the audience's imagination alongside (or even in place of) the actor's, these moments would have little power.

Ibsen, at the end of his plays, may also offer the actors only the simplest words: for example, in *Ghosts* and *John Gabriel Borkman*, 'the sun – the sun', and 'I love you, love you, love you.' Chekhov in his four major plays provides little scope for expressive action or speech at moments of greatest emotion. At the end of *Waiting for Godot*, Samuel Beckett gives the audience little more tangible or verbal drama than what it had heard and seen before.

These and other master dramatists have withdrawn from using their full resources of words or prescriptive actions when much has been at stake, so that it is the actor's imaginative identification with his or her character that must hold the play together and keep it moving forward. At these moments, in the absence of more being said or done, the audience can be more imaginately involved with the inner consciousness of the characters than elsewhere in the plays.

Perhaps an actor could, with advantage to the audience, withdraw further from expressive actions than is customary in theatres where he or she is encouraged to make the clear and outward expression of feeling the main attraction of each role undertaken. Instead of strong displays of emotion, actors could perhaps aim at imaginative involvement and a cool transparency in performance: such a borrowing would not be recognizable as an import, but an extension of a possibility that is already there.

'Importing' Modes of Improvisation

Another characteristic of Asian theatres is their reliance on improvisation. What happens at each moment is of that moment only; often performance is highly refined but nevertheless, to some degree, it will be unpredictable and unprecedented. No European or North American company works with such complex stage languages as the older traditional theatres of Asia, where distinctions between dance and acting, or between singing and speech, are almost impossible to draw, and this means that the same attitudes to improvisation are not readily applicable in the West. Nevertheless many productions do use complicated playtexts which demand great technical expertise in speech and performance, and here some experiments with improvisation might be productive.

Instead of spending a great deal of time working out ahead of performance how to play this line or that, what is the motive for this hesitation, or repetition, or image, what the cause of this change of address or peculiar syntax, how metre or phrasing should be given full value, it might be possible to delay decisions in these respects so that choice would depend almost entirely on the moment of playing. At least actors could be encouraged to improvise more than at present in these respects so that an audience will not get the impression that all decisions and choices have been made long before the performance.

Difficulties are obvious in recommending more improvisation in dealing with the technicalities of speech, not least because speech is only one aspect of a play's action. First, European theatres differ in that actors are required by their texts to interact with each other much more than in many forms of Asian theatre, where it is customary for a single actor to hold the stage alone for considerable periods of time and therefore play without referring to anyone else. Improvisation using western texts would have to depend on a high degree of mutual awareness between actors, which would either make its effect all the sharper or else encourage a wariness that would undermine the entire enterprise.

The second difficulty is that the actor would lose support of technically advanced and pre-programmed staging, since lighting, sound, and stage management would also have to be free to follow wherever the actor led. The risks and the possible gains of attempting a greater degree of improvisation would both be great.

In one respect, experiments with Asian theatre practice would raise so many difficulties that it must be considered impossible under present conditions in the West: there appears to be no way to give actors the same continuous involvement in their art as the performers in Kathakali or Kutiyattam, No or Kabuki. These Asian actors start training at the age of seven, and train every day with exercises that enhance the use of eyes, fingers, speech, and song, developing control and balance thoughout the whole body. Some of them are required to memorize many hours of drama to keep plays in the repertoire that take days to perform in full.

The other side of this strict and continuous regimen of training is a life that is centred in theatre. In India this can mean a lifetime spent in a temple and days full of devotion to the actor's art. How could actors concentrate upon theatre-making so totally in Europe or North America, and might they not cease to attract their audiences if they did so? How could they use all that time in the development of their art? Would any company have such confidence in the worth of their work as to require such devotion?

Doubly Invisible Exports

On return home, the theatre explorer has many questions to ask of his or her own theatre, especially in its essential elements that involve actors and audience. By trying to answer them honestly and then putting the tentative answers to the test of practice, thanks and respect can be best given to the theatres that provoked the interrogation of practice. No pillage will have been caused if nothing tangible is transported out of the society from which a theatre's life springs and by which it is possessed. Performances that result will speak for themselves without intrusive signposting of intercultural origin if the experiments are conducted with means already available in the traveller's own theatre.

Such doubly invisible exports – unseen on removal, and unrecognized when their consequences are on display – could, however, have further consequences beyond any theatre production. They might draw the two cultures closer together because, as their theatres begin to use the basic elements of performance in ways that are basically similar, so their audiences' sensibilities will be quickened in similar ways. From such a grounding, mutual understanding and exchanges might develop as naturally as light when it is allowed to possess more of its spectrum of colours.

Peter Brook has said that his experiments with intercultural theatre are aimed at discovering 'grace', a quality of performance which, 'since one must use words, one calls . . . "sacred".'[12] This suggests that his theatre seeks to display on stage a state of being that might be anywhere and everywhere. If such work were to renounce the outward signs of its origins and pay equal attention to the task of reflecting the lives of its own audiences, the invisible exports might be the means of staging local, contemporary, individual, and shared life so that it is all seen more piercingly and more enjoyably.

That difficult word 'sacred', with its implications of superiority and its loss of actuality, might then no longer be necessary or appropriate. By using overseas research to develop its own inheritance, a theatre might discover what it alone needs to create and encourage a more active and imaginative response from its local audience.

Ariane Mnouchkine believes that she has rediscovered the source of all theatre in the Orient, and her productions show that she has, indeed, led her actors to clearer and more eloquent performances. Granting this achievement, there seems little reason why she should dress those actors up in foreign clothes and give them actions which belong, unmistakably, to cultures that are out of the experience of her audiences and the cultural inheritance of her actors. Again, if exotic signs and trappings were renounced and attention focused at least as carefully on serving a local audience, an obvious and exclusive rarity might be exchanged for an attempt to present and transform the particular and unexampled lives from which this theatre takes its actual support.

Explorers of ancient Asian theatres have gained an opportunity to re-make their own by taking fuller advantage of what is potential in all theatre and responding to what is special in their own lives in this new and unprecedented age.

18

Notes and References

1. This article is a development of an earlier one, 'Theatrical Tourism', published in *Journal of Literature and Aesthetics* (Kollam, Kerala, India, 1997), V, i, p. 19-30. The kind permission of the editor is acknowledged with grateful thanks.

2. Interview in *Marie-Claire* (April 1986), quoted in *The Intercultural Performance Reader*, ed. Patrice Pavis (London; New York: Routledge, 1996), p. 97; and interview with Maria M. Delgado, in *In Contact with the Gods? Directors Talk Theatre*, ed. Maria M. Delgado and Paul Heritage (Manchester: Manchester University Press, 1996), p. 188.

3. *There Are No Secrets: Thoughts on Acting and Theatre* (London: Methuen, 1993), p. 22.

4. At Sadlers Wells Theatre, London, July 1994.

5. John Arden described the effect of a visit by a handful of academics to the Chhau dance-drama of Purulia in Bengal in *To Present the Pretence: Essays on the Theatre and its Public* (London; Methuen, 1977), p. 139-52.

6. Or, of course, puppets of various kinds manipulated by live persons.

7. Richard Schechner, *The Future of Ritual: Writings on Culture and Performance* (London: Routledge, 1993), p. 4-5.

8. This term is used significantly by Eugenio Barba in *Beyond the Floating Islands* (New York: Performing Arts Journal Publications, 1986).

9. 'Japanese Traces in Robert Wilson's Productions', *The Intercultural Performance Reader*, op. cit., p. 111. Visiting the Sopanam theatre company in Trivandrum, Kerala, in late 1995, the present writer met a young actor from Delhi who had spent a whole year learning the company's very active performance style, which is derived from local martial arts and Brahmin temple songs. This student could physically do all that was required of him when he was cast in one of the repertoire's plays, but had been unable to perform adequately in this assumed theatrical language – although the will to do so was strong, for he was seeking an alternative to the verbally-based styles that he had been taught previously and had found too limited.

10. *Theatre at the Crossroads of Culture*, trans. Loren Kruger (London; New York: Routledge, 1992), p. 202.

11. In June 1993, Keith Khan's *Moti Roti, Puttli Chunni*, drawing on Indian film and theatre as well as British theatre, was a huge success with multicultural audiences at the Theatre Royal, Stratford, in the East End of London. On the strength of this, Khan was commissioned to create another production two years later combining Trinidadian carnival with British theatre, to be premiered at the Royal Court in West London. But here audiences were small and unable to respond with pleasure to what was part of their daily lives.

12. Op. cit., p. 58-60.

Lizbeth Goodman, Tony Coe, Huw Williams

The Multimedia Bard: Plugged and Unplugged

The relationship between live theatre and the rapidly developing multimedia technologies has been ambiguous and uneasy, both in the practical and the academic arena. Many have argued that such technologies put the theatre and other live arts at risk, while others have seen them as a means of preserving the elusive traces of live performance, making current work accessible to future generations of artists and scholars. A few performance and production teams have entered the fray, deliberately pushing the technology to its limits to see how useful it may (or may not) be in dealing with the theatre. One such team – comprising Lizbeth Goodman, Tony Coe, and Huw Williams – forms the Open University BBC's Multimedia Shakespeare Research Project, and on 4 September 1997 they presented their work as the annual BFI Lecture at the Museum of the Moving Image on London's South Bank. What follows is an edited and updated transcript of the lecture – which was itself a 'multimedia performance' – intended to spark debate about the possibilities and limitations of using multimedia in creating and preserving 'live' theatre. Lizbeth Goodman is Lecturer in Literature at the Open University, where she chairs both the Shakespeare Multimedia Research Project and the new 'Shakespeare: Text and Performance' course. Tony Coe is Senior Producer at the OU/BBC, where Huw Williams was formerly attached to the Interactive Media Centre, before becoming Director of Createc for the National Film School, and subsequently Director of Broadcast Solutions, London. Together the team has created a range of multimedia CD-ROMs designed to test the limits and possibilities of new technologies for theatre and other live art forms – beginning with Shakespeare.

FIONA SHAW *is the main artistic associate for the Shakespeare Multimedia Project. We asked her the pivotal question: does Shakespeare work on CD-ROM?*

Fiona Shaw   I think Shakespeare *can* work on CD-ROM. The emphasis I suppose on CD-ROM, or on any screen Shakespeare, is that the context doesn't have to be set up in a way that plays into the narrative; that actually the deconstruction that seems to be happening in film and literature (and everything else) makes it very possible on CD-ROM to highlight the language – not in terms of helping the language to be exactly what it is, but to highlight it in a contrary way. I have found, just doing this video, that the picture is incredibly important; when the picture is doing so much work that you then don't have to make the words make the picture, but the words work in opposition. So, when Ken does his speech about drown-ing the steeples, the steeples don't have to be 'ye olde English' steeples: they can be suddenly a rather peculiar architectural construction that sits in the middle of a scene – they can be anywhere, anywhere, because film refuses to keep a frame, of the proscenium arch or whatever.

I think we're at a very, very interesting time when the problem with theatre and probably all performance is that it must deal with the new, with the next minute. And often the problem with Shakespeare in England is that every conceivable decorative form has already been investigated. So to find new meanings in a world where language is really dying in its written form and where film is absolutely on the rise as the new literature, you have now to find a way where you can clash the language with an image, so that somewhere it fuels the future, so that it's exciting by its combustion, not by its philosophical potential.

Fiona's words capture the essence or the spirit of our project. But we are very much aware of the pitfalls.

Intervening in the Debate

The cost of buying computing equipment capable of running high-speed CD-ROMs (compact discs designed to play back an impressive range of specially programmed audio-visual clips, and text from 'Read Only Memory' displayed on a computer screen) has decreased dramatically in the past few years, while the likelihood of accessing such equipment at local libraries and schools, universities, and businesses, has increased significantly. At the same time, a new generation of students has grown up using word processors and video games, and the barrier of 'technophobia' is being eradicated by generational shifts.

And the technology keeps on advancing. Meanwhile, Conservative government cuts to funding for the arts and education have left the live theatre behind the times. With venues closing and audiences dwindling, it has become increasingly important to revitalize the live theatre, and to protect and enhance the experience of community spectacle which the theatre can provide. The question is: can new technology help to keep theatre alive, or is it necessarily a threat, a replacement?

This is the question with which the OU/ BBC Shakespeare Multimedia Project began. As our work develops, we continue to seek feedback on the uses of new technological programmes designed specially for adult learners. So we needed to increase awareness of the products we have designed – to encourage people to use them and tell us what they think.

The 'set' is the Film Theatre at the Museum of the Moving Image. The seating, for around one hundred, is raked down to a bare-floor 'stage' area. This is backed by a full-wall projection screen, with a curtain at the rear. The exit is just by the stage area, to the right. Both curved walls of the space are flanked with TV monitors, which sometimes play in the full-screen image and sometimes play in alternative images. A podium is positioned in the stage area, left. A table set up with computers and various equipment is positioned in the stage area, right. Behind the curtain, the BBC crew's equipment is set up for audio-visual remix and playback facilities. The Control Room at the top back of the auditorium is set up for light control and cues. Outside the theatre, down the hall of the exhibition, is a reception area, where our 'stage directions' start . . .

Prequel

The performance begins during the wine and cheese reception at MOMI. Chris Palmer, Jenny Bardwell, and a BBC crew join Goodman, Coe, and Williams; they mingle with the guests and collect vox-pop 'talking head' responses to the informal questions: 'What do you think of Shakespeare?' and 'When did you first encounter Shakespeare?' The BBC crew leaves the reception five minutes early to allow time to cut and mix the vox-pops. The audience is invited to take their seats in the auditorium. House lights down.

Goodman, Coe, and Williams enter the auditorium from the side door, stage right, in black, and are introduced. Goodman stands at the podium, stage left, Coe and Williams sit at the table stage right (with the 'technology').

Cue sound   *Japanese drumming, from one of our* King Lear *recordings (low).*

Cue lights   *on screen, centre.*

Cue   *three-minute sequence of vox-pops recorded minutes earlier. This is intended to play as video with audio, but in the event one of the leads is faulty and only the sound plays in. After a few seconds pause, Goodman begins to deliver the lecture/performance anyway, aware of the irony of the 'multiple performances' and divided attention of the team, as Coe and Williams work to sort out the problem. The audience, interviewed afterwards, was not aware that there should have been video playback until Goodman joked about technology being unpredictable in live performance situations: the extra-scenic dynamic of lectures as well as performances is affected by the eventualities as well as intentions. The audience focused on the voices of the* *'vox-pops' and some commented on the class and generation differences in the voices, readable without visual cues. Some of our points had begun to make themselves, though we didn't know it at the time.*

1. Thirty Second (High) Culture

When I First Met Shakespeare [five minutes]

Main screen *Play in vox-pops recorded at reception. Tonight's audience give their informal views on and memories of Shakespeare [three minutes]. The range of replies includes a mix of the audience (who are surprised to hear themselves taking part in this lecture/performance), plus several A-level students, and directors and actors including Peter Sellars, Fiona Shaw, Ken Cranham, and Jude Akuwudike. The replies come from a range of people with different cultural perceptions and class backgrounds, of different races, genders, and generations.*

Some responses move on to address issues such as 'What can we learn from Shakespeare today?', 'How can we direct Shakespeare in new and exciting ways for audiences of today and tomorrow?', and 'How can we empower ourselves and our students in the process of learning about Shakespeare and performance?' There is space here for only a few sample responses, which we gained prior permission to print.

Ken Cranham The first time I was really attracted to Shakespeare I was taken by my school. We all went in a 'crocodile' down to the local cinema in Tulse Hill (from Tulse Hill Comprehensive – see, I've had a good background) to the cinema, and we saw Olivier's *Henry V*.

There used to be, after that, a cinema called the Academy in Oxford Street, which used to have an Olivier Shakespeare film season every year. I was always able to find someone who hadn't seen *Henry V* and I used to go every year. To me it's a very magical film; the sequence in the Globe Theatre where the camera is behind Olivier and he clears his throat and goes onto the stage to me is still one of the most thrilling things that I can remember or think about.

Brando and Olivier were my two acting heroes, and I thought Olivier in *Henry V* was transcendental. . . . I've got it on tape and it's still something I love to see.

Student 1 I've done *Romeo and Juliet* this year; we've been studying it all year and we've had our test on it at the end. So I was really interested in that and I enjoyed doing it. I've really enjoyed seeing *King Lear*, and it has made me extremely interested in Shakespeare.

Student 2 I'm pretty much the same as her. I'd like to find out more about Shakespeare. . . . I like reading it, but I like to see it performed as well.

Student 1 I prefer seeing it.

Fiona Shaw I was brought up in Cork, in Ireland, and we had Shakespeare on the syllabus. I think the first Shakespeare we did was *Julius Caeser*, which was a particularly unattractive piece as I had to assay the role of Brutus and I was not killed in the capitol. Subsequently we had a really boring series: we did *Richard II*, which I later found to be a much more interesting play than I did when I was little.

I think the play that I most liked at school was *Hamlet*. . . . I wrote an essay on *Hamlet* and found myself writing what was then the best essay I'd ever written because I suddenly 'got onto it'. But unlike, perhaps, most of the English people you've been interviewing, we didn't have much Shakespeare in Ireland, largely I think because when Spenser and Raleigh (who were contemporaries of Shakespeare) came over to Ireland they went down to West Cork where they made four hundred people jump into the sea with their armour on, and they ripped the pregnant women's stomachs out, and they hanged the priests.

So there's a real inherited resistance to Shakespeare's language and to all things Shakespearean in Ireland. It really wasn't until I went to drama school in London that I began to understand that this kind of much more muscular language was actually much more shared by Irish people than by English people today.

Jude Akuwudike   I heard a few quotations from my Dad – you know, he was constantly quoting Shakespeare. That was my first encounter: as a fount of wisdom, or whatever. And then at school, studying it at O-Level and A-Level, without a great deal of enjoyment – with some enjoyment, but the bawdy and all that kind of stuff seemed to be skirted around. So it never made full sense, it wasn't quite live, lively enough; it was something to be revered. I found greater joy in it after I'd left school and came to know myself, and I could make up my own mind about what I felt about it, and found that really nothing was forbidden in Shakespeare.

Like Ken was saying – he encountered it in *Henry V* – there's another generation, I think, that first encountered Shakespeare in Franco Zeffirelli's *Romeo and Juliet* – particularly identifying with Mercutio. It kind of fired up everything in you about what this thing is about. Really pretty exciting – fun and exciting – yes!

These words were followed by one last 'vox-pop' from Jenny Bardwell, one of our BBC producers. Jenny's voice was Goodman's cue. As the last vox-pop ended, lights rose on the podium and technology table, and a spotlight on the podium allowed Goodman to address the audience 'live' in a continuation of the introduction, as the audience was invited to shift seamlessly from recorded to 'real-time' lecture mode.

2. Plugged and Unplugged

[*Two minutes*]

Cue   *lights up on Goodman for Introduction.*

Goodman   In this presentation we're going to address some of the questions raised in our informal 'vox-pop' interviews, and hopefully some of the questions and concerns of the rest of the audience as well. We've done our best to include some of you in the presentation already. While this is hardly a

creative and deliberate participation on your part, it's the closest thing to interactivity we could get in this setting this evening.

In the next hour, we'll address a number of buzz words and phrases, explaining our approaches to them:

- Shakespeare plugged and unplugged (the dilemma of distance teaching of performance)
- Shakespeare in multimedia
- Reinventing the Bard
- Reaching distant audiences
- Creating 'virtual' classrooms and 'interpretive communities'
- Learning with and through new technologies

We'll take you behind the scenes of the Shakespeare Multimedia Project to explain how and why three people from different backgrounds joined forces to devise teaching tools which allow new technology to help the student get to grips with language, image, sound, and the learning process. We'll demonstrate the learning curve we've all also experienced, as we've unlearned some of the skills of our respective trades and learned new ways of thinking and working, in order to collaborate as fully as possible in a project concerned with empowering students through prioritizing their, not our, ideas and imaginations.

The Shakespeare Multimedia Research Project has only been operating as such since November 1995, but our concerns with finding ways to make the teaching of drama more interactive began several years earlier, when we were working primarily with video, TV and audio performances. What we've learned this year is the subject of our talk today.

We'll show you extracts from several videos and two prototype CD-ROMs we've produced so far, and some new material in progress as well, aspects of which will be integrated into a new suite of three fully functional interactive CD-ROMs on *King Lear in Performance* (in progress).

3. Lizbeth's Lament

Shakespeare Unplugged
and (Long) Distance Teaching [*four minutes*]

By 'Shakespeare unplugged' we mean live performance, performed for an audience in a shared space. The key concerns of live performance include: possibilities and problems of sharing with large, distant audiences; possibilities of sharing performances, like books, with international audiences; issues involved in assessment; the desire to keep up with new technology at least in so far as students are increasingly using it. We can't offer teaching tools of a truly empowering nature if we aren't up to date with the skills students are learning elsewhere in their lives.

The use of new technology in teaching about performance is essential, particularly for those of us who work for the UK's leading distance teaching institution, the Open University. Thousands of students across the UK and Europe, and increasingly in North America, Asia, and Africa, use each video 'lecture' and multimedia performance tool. The effect is the creation of an international 'virtual classroom' – a massively successful and radically expanded version of Harold Wilson's idea of a 'University of the Air'.

To keep the Open University, and access to education, truly 'open', we need to increase access – to provide all students with equal access to the equipment, the tools, and the skills to make use of these new opportunities for study. To ensure that the arts are taught as well as the better-funded sciences, and in addition to the largely self-funding business programmes, we also need to ensure that we place emphasis on the possibilities for learning about the arts in and through multimedia.

For me personally – due to my own very poor vision, but also to my background of work with children of limited sight and hearing – educational objectives are fuelled by a desire to expand 'literature' to include the study of non-spoken and non-written 'texts' and forms of communication; to open out the possibilities of education in the arts to people of many different abilities; and to offer entry points and learning paths for deaf, blind, immobile, and geographically-isolated students as well as for those who can and do go out and experience 'live' theatre in all its richness and variety.

All this work must aim to make learning fun, to get past the idea that OU and other university courses must involve 'experts' on screen or at podiums talking out at, not to or with, those who are enrolled in a course. So we try to emphasize the possibilities of performance for learning about learning, about the ways in which we all follow individual paths through our educational and imaginative experiences.

We can't reach these pedagogic goals if we treat Shakespeare plays as texts. We must also consider performance possibilities – not just Shakespeare on film, but also live performance – always acknowledging that we must use new technologies to help us 'cheat' so as to try to create some sense of the process behind any given theatre production. In this way, students and users of the CD-ROMs will be empowered to enact and pursue their own learning paths, and to use creative thinking as well as intellect.

This empowerment of the student is our large educational aim. We know we must find ways to entertain and amuse, too. And one powerful way to entertain and amuse is through engagement with Shakespeare's plays themselves – in performance.

Cue   *Japanese drumming.*

Cue   *Lights down on podium, up stage left and in left corridor to stage.*

Cue actors   *Two student actors from RADA enter, Clare Bloomer as Lady Macbeth from behind screen, Neil D'Souza as Macbeth from the rear left of the auditorium.*

4. Performance: Macbeth

Act II, Scene ii, lines 15-56 [*three minutes*]

Cue   *Lights from white to blue.*

MACBETH   I have done the deed. . . .
LADY MACBETH   Ay!

MACBETH   Hark! . . .

  Raise lights (red) centre stage.

LADY MACBETH   Infirm of purpose!

  Lights from red to blue.

LADY MACBETH (*exiting stage right*)   . . . I'll guild
  the faces of the grooms withall, for
  it must seem their guilt. . . .

  *Sound and lights: bring up drums softly,
  actors freeze, fade lights to black, actors exit
  stage right on drum beats.*

Goodman   That was Shakespeare 'unplugged' – Neil D'Souza and Clare Bloomer in a
scene from *Macbeth*, recently directed by Bill
Gaskill for RADA. But what if we 'plug
Shakespeare in' – that is, capture it in some
recorded form?

5. What's All This about the Plug?

Tony talks back [three minutes]

Coe   Live performance is great, but how do
you discuss it meaningfully with someone
who wasn't there? Recording performance
gets around that, to some extent.

Image 1   *from a Cheek by Jowl performance
of a scene from* As You Like It, *included on the*
As You Like It *video in the 'Approaching
Literature' series* (OU/BBC, 1995).

That was a brief extract from Cheek by
Jowl's 1995 all-male production of *As You
Like It*. We can all talk about that performance extract; we can send it out in a
video to people who aren't here, we can
watch it at different times. We've turned the
performance into a text – a filmic or tele-
visual one – and in the process we've 'fixed'
it: captured one interpretation and made
that a 'set text' of sorts for shared reference.

  In choosing one version over any of
the multiple possible other versions, we've
changed its meaning, or its set of potential
meanings – whether it's a stage performance
recorded on the night, or (as in the Cheek by
Jowl version) a performance re-directed for
the camera; whether it is a version specifically staged for television or a version shot
and edited on film. In every case, after the

performers have had their say, the camera
director, the lighting camera-operator, and
the picture editor all add their own meanings to the original performances, which in
most cases are recorded or filmed piecemeal
and out of sequence anyway.

  On the small screen and the large screen
your gaze is directed: the close up, the wide
shot, the zoom, the pan: everything in the
frame may (and usually does) have a
particular significance. You cannot let your
eyes wander as you can at a live performance. Your capacity as a spectator to remake
the meaning of a scene is almost totally
constrained.

  And yet the power and reach of recorded
performance is huge. The problem we face
in recording Shakespeare for distant audiences is: how can we allow an audience the
freedom of the live performance dynamic
while using recorded performance? Is there
a way to empower the viewer, a way of
seeing how the process of making performance leads to creating meaning?

6. But What about New Media?

Huw's Hyperboles [three minutes]

Williams   We've now watched examples
of Shakespeare 'plugged' and 'unplugged'.
But multimedia allows us to go further and
to combine approaches, using new technologies to 'get at' the arts, encouraging students
to engage with the processes involved and
choices made as any team of artists works
towards a given performance. We wanted to
combine 'plugged' and 'unplugged' approaches so that students using the CD-ROMs
would have a greater degree of choice in
determining the kinds of performances to be
studied, what those performances might
sound and look like, what meanings they
might have or hold for particular viewers
in particular places and cultures, at different
times, working for different reasons, at different points in their careers or studies.

  There isn't yet a truly useful and comprehensive term for the kind of work we
want to do: not 'plugged', not 'unplugged',
but maybe 'hyperplugged' or 'hotwired'?

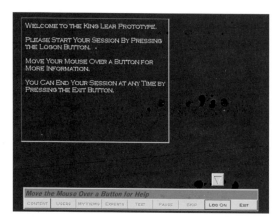

We've talked about all these terms as we've worked. Whatever the term for it, the result is a set of CD-ROMs aimed at maximizing student interest in the dynamics of live performance, using multimedia technologies to create an interface between ideas, images, and words.

Here are the screen designs for the demo and pilot CD-ROMS:

Image 2   *Screen design, from* As You Like It *demo CD-ROM.*

Image 3   *Screen design, from* King Lear *pilot CD-ROM (above).*

The 'As You Like It' in Performance' demo CD-ROM uses a fairly linear format of exercises leading up to the 'pay-off exercise' which allows students to cut their own version of a scene. The 'King Lear in Performance' pilot CD-ROM uses more of a Web structure, where users may enter or exit the programme at different points and may follow any number of loops through the materials. This is more of a resource disk, offering backstage views of the rehearsal process for several different staged productions, with a 'pay-off' exercise allowing users to position the camera differently to frame their own preferred performances, or to edit together different staged performances of the same scene.

Both CD-ROMs were put together very quickly as 'research and development' projects, in order to test the limits and possibilities of the technology in the teaching of Shakespeare with regard to live performance.

The new suite of CD-ROMs now in progress builds on the work put into the demo and pilot, and on a wide range of feedback collected from teachers, students, actors, directors, and designers in the UK and USA.

Goodman   We'll discuss the CD-ROMs in more detail in a moment, but first it might help if we outline the main pedagogic idea which fuelled both of these CD-ROMs and all the associated videos we've recorded in the past few years.

7. Blowing the Fuse

Text, Image, Ideas [six minutes]

Cue lights   *on podium, technology table, and house lights as well,*

Goodman   In any creative team, a range of priorities and concerns will be raised, and at the worst of times these may cause conflict and may lead to friction in the process, adversely affecting the product: the work. We decided from the outset to work as a small team, with the core (the three of us) coming from distinct but overlapping areas of expertise. Our three sets of perspectives equally informed the working process, as did the collective experience which emerged as we each started from one position but found that our ways of working complemented each other's, and that what we could create was something new.

Huw Williams started out with academic degrees in human geography and computer technologies, moved into advertising, then into interactive media design and programming. He had an avid interest in performance but had not done much work on the theatre in relation to multimedia before he joined our team.

Tony Coe trained in drama and maintains an interest in the theatre (he recently performed, for instance, in the premiere of Bryony Lavery's new play *Ophelia*, discussed in Jane de Gay's article in a forthcoming issue of *NTQ*), but the focus of his work for the past twenty-odd years has been the recording of plays for audio, TV, and video

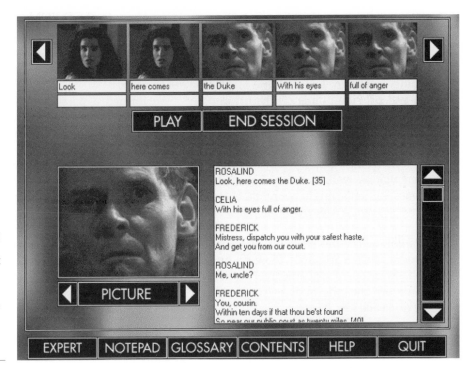

Look here comes the Duke With his eyes full of anger

PLAY   END SESSION

ROSALIND
Look, here comes the Duke. [35]

CELIA
With his eyes full of anger.

FREDERICK
Mistress, dispatch you with your safest haste,
And get you from our court.

ROSALIND
Me, uncle?

FREDERICK
You, cousin.
Within ten days if that thou be'st found
So near our public court as twenty miles. [40]

◄ PICTURE ►

EXPERT NOTEPAD GLOSSARY CONTENTS HELP QUIT

Opposite page: opening screen for the *King Lear* pilot CD-ROM.

Right: from the 'Cast Your Own' section of the *As You Like It* demo.

production, mediating between text, sound, and image.

I started from a divided perspective: as an academic concerned with scholarly research and distance teaching, I found that my theatre background and experience of working with disabled children helped me to translate issues of 'access' in performance, using invented languages and making connections between text, images, and ideas. For me, all this work is about showing that the assumption of linear development in teaching or thinking can be queried.

None of us is stuck in one way of working or thinking, nor do we expect that all our students or users of these CD-ROMs will all follow the same paths through, or arrive at the same ends. It's all about finding ways to replace words with images and movements and sounds and design features on screen – but the work, the words and text, had to go in, in order that the empowerment could begin for the students or users of the product. The visual element is very important to us all, as is a concern for including process (rehearsal, workshop, etc.) as well as the finished product – whether plugged or unplugged . . . or 'fused'.

We brought these aims together in our *As You Like It* video, produced in 1994-95.[1] There, for the first time, we decided to shift focus from the process between actors and director to include students on camera, to invite viewers and students into the learning process. Here's an extract from a video we made earlier. . . .

Cue *Fade lights, stage and house, to black – and bring up Fiona Shaw introducing the* As You Like It *video.*

8. A Prototype Virtual Classroom

As You Like It *on video [six minutes]*

Goodman In one of the extracts, Fiona Shaw teaches students from LAMDA to find the weight and value of language, through a coin exercise in which each phrase in Rosalind and Celia's verbal exchange is assigned a point, represented by a coin. Fiona shows the students how language can be weighed, how characters find their relationship to each other first through the words of the play and then through movement and interpretation (as in later exercises on the video).

27

In years gone by, teachers might have spoken to us through TV or the frame of the video, but only recently has the OU/BBC begun to include the students' experiences of learning on screen: to frame the learning process and provide points of identification on the screen for students at home. We went in an exciting new direction by using these students in the frame – and that's a road we're still going down. But feedback indicated that as well as being included in the frame, students might want to change the frame, to have power over the image.

Coe   This is when the need for interactive multimedia became apparent. Here's a bit of demo CD-ROM we made earlier, very quickly and relatively cheaply, from existing video footage of *As You Like It*.

9. Demonstrating Shakespeare

Approaching As You Like It [*ten minutes*]

Cue   *Huw Williams brings up the* As You Like It *demo CD-ROM full screen, opens the 'Expert' section, and plays in an extract of Fiona Shaw.*

Goodman   Fiona appears on location in St. Pancras; she was recorded as we rehearsed for the version of the banishment scene included on this CD-ROM. She sits informally in the foreground and allows us to see, behind her, the cameras, the smoke machine, the scaffolding, the boom operators, the actors reading their lines, and the producer talking to the stills photographer.

Many other experts are available on the CD-ROM to share their views, their unique perspectives on the play, or on the processes of staging and recording Shakespeare. But the real impact of the CD-ROM lies in the interactivity – the invitation to students to play along.

On the CD-ROM, we started with a desire to do the impossible, in order to enable our students to do the impossible. We heard everyone telling us that programmes which allowed full interactivity and recutting scenes just wouldn't work. We heard that the technology had not yet been invented, that the production difficulties would prove insurmountable, and that in any case the learning objectives of such a strategy would not be clear.

We formed a pact to prove the sceptics wrong. Like Macbeth's three witches, we stirred the cauldron of warnings, but we found ideas and inspiration in the bubbly brew. We sketched out our own storyboard, designed a frame, went back to the drawing board (or the cauldron) again and again. By trial and error and long hard slog we found a formula that worked for all three of us – and we then set out to implement it, in the hope that if our three sets of objectives, standards of originality, and excellence could be met, then there should be something of value in what we produced for a wide range of students and users.

Huw and his team of 'techies' designed us some new software and screen interfaces; Tony and his crew found ways to make the limitations of our existing video footage work to our advantage; I wrote and rewrote and rewrote until the balance of image, word, and text, and of teaching and interactive entertainment, seemed to be about right. We were on our way.

The biggest challenge from an academic point of view was thinking through all the possibilities of interactivity and exercises on point of view, or perspective. This is a tricky issue to teach in live theatre, but is horrendously (and wonderfully) complicated when the video camera and computer screen intervene between 'audience' and 'performance'.

Designing the alternative cuts of our Banishment scene involved thinking about images, positions of the actors, camera angles, which characters are in frame and which are not . . . and also thinking about the relationship between text and image. Those who are more comfortable with text might start by clicking on family words, to see that the shot changes occur on those words. Those who are more familiar with visual thinking or lateral thinking might like to identify moments when the shot changes or when a 'pivotal point' occurs, and go to the text to see what's happening there.

To do this exercise we needed to work from our aims in reverse, to set up all the skills required to achieve that aim in writing the overall script for the CD-ROM. We first decided what we wanted the user to be empowered to do, then worked backwards, offering all the definitions, tutorial advice, and techniques necessary to help 'users' to succeed through guided 'distance' teaching in a pre-programmed form.

We provided exercises on identifying shot changes, reading the scene from the play, and working with an annotated edition (in this case, the latest Arden), identifying and naming camera angles and shots, identifying 'pivotal points' where action meets text to create meaning in some unique or important way, combining text and images in alternative versions (a gender cut, a family cut) to demonstrate the different interpretations available in any given production: all this leading up to the final 'pay-off' activity of the 'Cut Your Own' exercise whereby students can move selected still images to match lines of text, creating their own storyboards which can be played on the computer and printed off for use in tutorials or in staging.

What I found liberating about this first demo CD-ROM was the way in which users seemed willing to criticize immediately. The usual intimidation of teaching in printed form was refreshingly displaced by this interactive media format. Using the mouse was not seen as an unusual way to interact with performance, and no one I spoke to seemed to object to being asked to form opinions and make creative decisions about the play, or to using the technology to share their vision with others.

The focus on demystifying the process seemed right. By including interviews with the cast and crew and by showing the 'joins', taking the camera backstage and into empty spaces, showing the smoke machine in frame, etc., students did seem to get a better sense of *why* they found performance interesting. I was delighted to find that students and teachers alike were quick to say which performance versions, cuts, and ideas they liked and didn't like, and why.

What I found frustrating was the way in which the CD-ROM format seemed to remove pedagogy to the margins. Replacing textual teaching with image and audio-based teaching is fine, so long as there are clear teaching points available (albeit 'layered' out of sight) which users can return to when they wish. I quite enjoyed displacing the conventional teacher–student relationship, discovering the 'joins' of that power relationship, and inverting the power so that students were empowered to make choices and decisions.

I also enjoyed working collaboratively, sharing ideas and resources with colleagues to produce teaching tools. But I felt that students could have been better prepared to argue through their choices on the CD-ROM if they had more tutorial advice along the way. Some would ignore this, of course, but some would benefit from it enormously – and the best distance teaching offers levels to make the work accessible to the widest variety of students. Making this CD-ROM was a learning process for me, too. The non-linear nature of this medium (or combination of media) for teaching suited me well, as did the concept of working with the senses, with opening up 'windows' for the imaginative use of others.

The script for this CD-ROM had to be rewritten several times as the process of getting the ideas on screen in an interactive form required replacing words with images, exercises, graphics, video, or audio whenever possible. It was excellent training to work backwards, offering tools to lead the student/user through and enable empowerment of individuals, having to stop and think myself into the shoes and senses of every possible user.

Of course the result is partial, and only partially successful, but I hoped that we were on to something which was as much to do with the way people learn as it was about Shakespeare or performance.

Coe So, for a few minutes we were all rather pleased with ourselves. . . .

Williams Until we collected feedback. . . .

29

10. Interlude

BBC crew led by Chris Palmer play in a wide range of soundbites and 'vox-pops' collected as feedback in response to the question: 'Does Shakespeare work in multimedia?'

Goodman The responses to this question varied enormously, as we might expect. Fiona Shaw (quoted at the start of this article) is most confident about the uses of multimedia for Shakespeare and theatre more generally, but then she has had the experience of working on the CD-ROMs with us. I was more suspicious about the technology, its uses and possible abuses, before I began to work with the media and found that it is possible to use the media without allowing it to 'use you'.[2]

Each user of the CD-ROM found things which worked and things which seemed worrying. . . . It is the nature of multimedia that it should appeal to different people at different levels, not all of which can be easily rationalized or explained. We end the 'Cut Your Own Section' of the *As You Like It* demo CD-ROM with a comic warning to users: 'Some of the critics loved your work; some hated it.' We wanted here to remind those who use the CD-ROM that they have created an interpretation, open to further interpretation and criticism from 'armchair' critics, other students, and teachers. In that same spirit, we want to round off our presentation by responding to some criticisms of our own work.

11. Critique Your Own Shakespeare!

[Four minutes]

Coe It was while Amanda Willett was working with Fiona Shaw cutting together a final version of the *As You Like It* banishment scene (directed by Fiona for video) that we glimpsed just how we might begin to empower the CD-ROM user and provide some sense of the performance process. Amanda and Fiona went through several different 'cuts' before settling on the one we've called 'The Director's Cut' on the CD-ROM. In

recording these and any scenes, it's necessary to shoot more versions or takes of a given scene than you might eventually need, so you often end up with several different versions of the same dialogue. Obviously the costumes, sets, actors, crew, and director are the same, but the performances can (and often do) vary, with different inflections, nuances, emphases, and so on. The shots can vary considerably too. Here's an example:

Image 4 *Four images of the Duke's entrance: (a) two shot; (b) low angle wide shot; (c) mid shot; and (d) close up.*

Coe The same line of dialogue, covering the Duke's entrance, was shot as a two shot of Celia and Rosalind running out of frame, as a very distant low angle wide shot up the stairs as the Duke descended, as a mid shot of the Duke, and several different close ups as he entered and spoke his first line. In the editing process, these various shots are combined to produce the final 'performance'.

What we realized as we worked our way through four cuts was that each one gave certain aspects of the scene a slightly different emphasis. So while a wide low angle shot of the Duke tended to emphasize his political power, a huge close up emphasized his direct personal involvement. By combining the same words with different images, different meanings could be generated from the same bank of available images.

Furthermore, if you approached this process wanting to convey a particular idea about character (wanting to present the Duke as a political leader rather than a 'family man', for instance) that could then directly and usefully inform the shots you would choose, the points in the dialogue where you would change shot, and, most crucially, the order of shots you would use and the developing narrative effect of shot succeeding shot.

We decided that if we could offer this facility through CD-ROM, each user could generate their very own version of the scene, and so within the constraints of the original material make their own meaning for that scene. This approach could not teach users of the CD-ROM to be apprentice editors or directors, but it could give them a very clear personal experience of how meaning can be created and altered within certain absolute parameters.

Having chosen our approach to the CD-ROM, we also had to address the problem of how to help users whose experience of the technology might vary considerably. Almost everything else we decided to include was selected for one of two reasons: either to equip users with the necessary skills to work the 'cut-your-own' option, or to frame the interactive exercises on this CD-ROM in wider practical and theoretical contexts. We also determined that these learning processes should be as interactive as possible.

Goodman The interactive exercises were developed accordingly. Fiona's original cut of the banishment scene was included in the first of what I tend to call the 'interactivities'; there, we first asked users to identify the number of shot changes in the scene, asking students/users to develop the skill of careful observation, of looking to see when the shot has changed or when what is seen has been framed by a decision made by a director or editor.

Coe By clicking the mouse button each time they see a cut, students/users register their responses on a timeline which appears below the video window and which is automatically scored by the computer program. This kind of introductory 'interactivity' is perfect for CD-ROM because there is an undeniable, exact answer. There are 23 shot changes in the scene, including the one that almost no one gets: the four frame shot when the Duke slaps Celia.

Image 5 *Four frames of the tricky shot of the Duke slapping Celia.*

Coe Another major interactive exercise is the 'Pivotal Points' game, in which we ask the students/users to decide for themselves on several pivotal points in the scene which seem 'pivotal' or particularly important – moments where the action/mood changes

significantly. We ask students to look closely at how the relationship between the words and images, and the succession of images, worked around these pivotal points. There is a very detailed tutorial system layered into the CD-ROM: students can ask for basic advice or very detailed advice and appropriate tutorial comments by Lizbeth will be played, with visual and audio examples.

The next stage was to present users with an 'alternative' version of the scene, to ask them to try and identify how the meaning of the scene had been changed and to show that there is no single 'right' version. In this case we selected the Gender/Power cut. The setting, the actors, and the director remained the same, but the scene was re-edited, sometimes with the same shots, sometimes using new shots, but most importantly cutting them together differently.

In the Gender/Power cut, then, a different mood was established from the outset as the Duke eavesdrops on Celia and Rosalind's intimate conversation with his sinister lord and Touchstone – whom we then find has been eavesdropping on the whole scene! A combination of low angle wide shots up the huge staircase reveals Celia and Rosalind's point of view of the Duke, while huge close-ups establish a direct connection between the Duke (wielder of power) and the young women (oppressed by gender and by their lower position in the frame).

These power relations are emphasized by deliberate cuts away from Rosalind as she makes her impassioned defence. Although we still hear her words, we see the Duke putting his boots on, slamming the heel down to get them on properly. Users are then directed to look closely at how the pivotal points they identified in the director's cut are treated in this version.

Under the 'Help' button there is more explicit information about what to watch out for. In Version 2, for example – the Family Cut – many shot changes occur on family words – father, sister, cousin, uncle – and the shots concentrate on the three family members almost exclusively. In Version 3, the Gender/Power cut, shot changes occur on words which denote power and authority –

liege, highness, Duke – and the shots involve other characters, making this a much more overtly public scene.

The CD-ROM also features an 'Expert' button. Practitioners including Juliet Stevenson, Deborah Warner, Fiona Shaw, Dan Chumley (of the San Francisco Mime Troop), and Peter Sellars provide brief moments of encouragement and enlightenment.

Image 6 *'Help' functions at bottom of* As You Like It *screen* (*see page 27*).

Goodman The 'Glossary' button contains a general glossary of drama terms, a glossary of film terms, and textual notes on the scene, along with a 'Notepad' function allowing the user to make notes while working through the various components of the CD-ROM. These notes can be saved and printed off, to be used as primary material, as the basis for an essay, or in directing the scene on stage. But the most popular feature is the 'Cut Your Own' interactivity.

Williams Finally we arrive at *your* version of the scene. For the *As You Like It* CD-ROM we developed an animation storyboarding technique which places still frame images against an actual soundtrack, so that users can produce their own individualized cuts of the first thirty seconds of this scene. Why only thirty seconds? Because the possibilities for combining images and words are so numerous that we thought we'd better limit the exercise.

Some prefer 'traditional' cuts such as match, for instance, a close up of the Duke's face and eyes to the lines: 'Look, here comes the Duke/With his eyes full of anger.' But not me. I prefer the experimental approach. Here's my favourite Tarantino cut, using close ups in unpredictable ways which may seem to cut against the meaning of the scene (but whatever you do is okay, so long as you can explain your choices if Lizbeth or some other academic asks for justification).

Image 7 *Close up on fist from* As You Like It *CD-ROM.*

Williams Cutting your own scene doesn't stop there. The result can be played back full screen, saved onto your own floppy, sent down the line to another person – a tutor perhaps – and even be printed off in black and white, to keep.

Great! But that wasn't exactly what I'd been hoping for . . . or so I thought. At that point (in late 1995) it seemed that the real Holy Grail was to be able to cut your own scene with full-screen, full-motion video. Even as we first demonstrated the *As You Like It* prototype CD-ROM, we were already planning and setting up recording for the next one – a new version of *King Lear* which used specially shot performances rather than scavenged out-takes.

Of course demonstration means feedback! Constructive criticism!

Coe The main criticism of the CD-ROM was that it seemed to be about teaching the student/user to be an editor or director. For us that's not true: it's a tool for teaching about process, showing just some of the parameters that affect and produce meaning in a recorded performance. There was also a feeling that we hadn't addressed in enough detail issues like the way lighting, costume, and set affect meaning.

So we decided to do a new CD-ROM which would use stage lighting (though we knew how difficult this would be to digitize) and which would compare theatre spaces and consider the problems actors face in performing to live audiences and for the camera. For this version, we wanted a different form of 'Cut Your Own' exercise, to highlight the position of the camera in the space.

Goodman To try and deal with all these points we decided to record three different versions of the storm scene on the heath ('Blow winds . . . ') from *King Lear*. We set our colleagues at the University of Alberta the task of selecting three different groups of designers/directors/actors to see whether we could demonstrate/record the entire process from first reading of the text through the rehearsals, set construction, lighting design, and final performance.

12. Piloting Shakespeare

King Lear [*ten minutes*]

Goodman Our second 'production' was the *King Lear in Performance* pilot CD-ROM.[3] We began work on this as we gave out the first demos of the previous CD, trying it out on students and staff in North America. We made several trips to Canada and the USA, and gave a series of demos throughout the UK. Each time we did a demo we collected feedback, informally at first.[4]

By the time we were ready to shift focus to the pilot CD-ROM on *King Lear*, we had outlined the new performance and master-class materials we'd gathered to address that criticism, and had decided to structure the new CD-ROM entirely differently – in a Web style, so that the CD would function as a resource disk, rather than in the more linear style of the demo CD – and shift the focus from technical issues about identifying shots and manipulations of images to the technical issues which shape live performance. We decided, then, to focus on the process of making theatre: on the impact of the choice of a playing space, set, design, costume and

colour scheme, and the major impact of light in live performance.

Here, we set ourselves an entirely new task. Rather than using all the best video images we could find and working with the light parameters to get the best digital image possible, we set out to record in 'live theatre' conditions, with stage rather than film lighting. We knew that we would lose a lot in picture quality, but that this would be part of the learning process, for us and for users – the most visible evidence that live theatre must be seen live to be fully appreciated.

With these potential problems and limitations in mind, we decided to try for the impossible again, and set about our recordings with two new aims added to the list: we would design a new program to allow us to play in full-screen, full-motion video images of our new performances, and we would work on improving the accessibility of the screen for users of many levels of ability.

Huw Williams explains the differences between the first 'Cut Your Own' version on the *As You Like It in Performance* demo CD-ROM and the further development of the *King Lear in Performance* pilot CD-ROM, which pushed technology to the limit with full-screen and full-motion video, using that

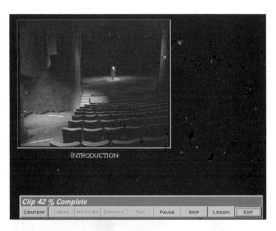

INTRODUCTION

Clip 42 % Complete

CONTENT | USERS | MY VIEWS | EXPERTS | TEXT | PAUSE | SKIP | LOGON | EXIT

technology to create a different kind of 'Cut Your Own' Shakespeare.

Williams This time the 'Cut Your Own' option was rather different. It allowed the user to choose between different full-motion performances of the same thirty seconds of the scene. The user could choose the camera position, and either stick to it all through the thirty seconds or change it for another position at two predetermined points. Not only could this be done for each of the three different performances, but it was also made possible for the user to choose between the different performances, cutting them together at the sync points. This can create interesting effects, though it was more of an experiment than a teaching strategy . . .

Goodman And we're not sure it has been successful pedagogically. That option may remain on one of the new suite of CD-ROMs but only as an optional exercise about sight-lines and perspective. The more interactive 'Cut Your Own' version will be reinstated as one of the primary teaching exercises.

On this CD-ROM, though, the 'Cut Your Own' exercise is less integral to the total learning 'package'. It is there as one way of bringing ideas together and testing theory against practice, but here a range of other exercises are equally important. The pilot CD-ROM on *King Lear* includes much more rehearsal and performance material, which means that there are more variables and more to think about and assess. Still, the most exciting developments were the integ-

ration of performance materials on design and the fact that we were able to move from the more linear development of the *As You Like It* menu to a more lateral or Web design, with any number of entry points, but always with performance at the centre.

Also, for me, the integration of communication issues at the centre of one of the performances reinforced the idea that interactive multimedia performances can help us learn about communicative gestures, and ways of learning and teaching. With time only to hit the highlights, here's what the thing can do:

Cue *Full screen: bring up and play in the Introduction to the CD-ROM. Play in Goodman walking down the raked auditorium of the University of Alberta Timms Centre Theatre, and up onto the stage* (left).

Goodman (*on screen*)   No other medium can create, much less rival, the excitement of live theatre. The excitement of being part of the audience gives you a direct connection to a play, and to the actors, all taking part in a performance in a shared space. On this CD-ROM, we want to create some of that sense of excitement for you. We'll take you onto different stages/different stages/different stages/different stages/different stages . . .

Several stages appear behind Goodman: proscenium arch, black box, raked, studio, RADA, etc. The cuts are quick – almost MTV style – so that this is less a traditional academic link than an invitation to look at stage spaces from different angles while the basic introductory information is conveyed.

. . . different playing spaces, with different sets, costumes, actors, designs, LIGHTS.

Spot appears on Goodman, centre stage.

We'll take you behind the scenes to see the workings of the theatre, and will invite you to step up to the lens of the video camera as well.

Perspectives seen from these vantage points.

We'll encourage you to see and interact with a range of scenes from different spaces in the audience, and from the actor's point of view as well. From this playing space, here's what an actor can see from here, and here, and here, and here. . .

Cut to Goodman in audience, spots in different positions.

Where you go is up to you.

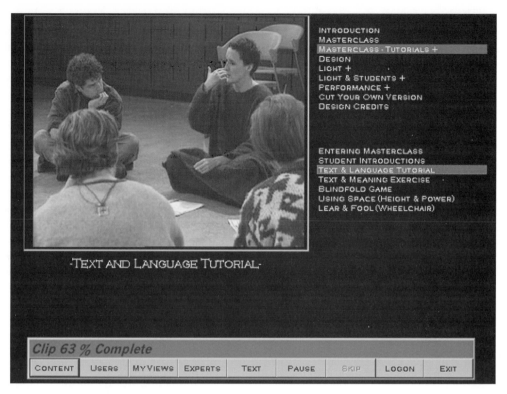

-TEXT AND LANGUAGE TUTORIAL-

Clip 63 % Complete

| CONTENT | USERS | MY VIEWS | EXPERTS | TEXT | PAUSE | SKIP | LOGON | EXIT |

Goodman This introduction leads the user into a number of those 'different spaces' for performance, several of which were used in the three storm scenes for the CD-ROM. Special features of this CD-ROM include:

- Three new performances of a scene from the play with 'recut' options
- Latest Arden text with scholarly notes
- Masterclass with Fiona Shaw
- Full audio performance of the play, directed by Fiona Shaw
- New version of the scene directed by Fiona Shaw, in collaboration with RADA
- Optional tutorial sessions
- Over twenty interactive exercises on performance and design
- Experts in the field responding to key critical and practical issues
- Built-in feedback option, allowing the user to become part of a 'virtual audience' or community of scholars
- Sign language interpretation as an optional text, or optional performance

Opposite page: Goodman on stage at the University of Alberta, introducing the *King Lear in Performance* CD-ROM. Above: Fiona Shaw conducting a masterclass with Canadian students.

Williams This CD-ROM also features a feedback option: the student/user may type in her or his views, ideas, and responses, thus becoming part of the 'virtual audience' and community of scholars, and adding to the database on the CD-ROM itself.

It presents and analyses new performances of Shakespeare, including design and directing elements, with an interactive base leading to the editing of selected scenes, which can be printed off in storyboard form by the student/user.

Goodman This CD-ROM also works with issues of disability, by including one version of the heath scene from *King Lear* featuring a profoundly deaf actor as Fool, and offering variations on image with text, or image with signing. The play's theme of communication is thus highlighted in and through performance, and the student/user interacts with a range of communicative languages.

The basic design/flow model can be outlined as follows:

Module 1
Introduction and Masterclass
(from page to stage)

Module 2   *Module 3*
Design   Performance

Module 4
Edit Your Own

Contents

Help

Glossary
(*terminology of live performance
and of video performance*)

Arden III Text and Scholarly Notes

Notebook

Experts

Feedback

To begin as a student in a virtual workshop situation, users can follow the students at the University of Alberta into their masterclass with Fiona Shaw.

Image 8 *Fiona Shaw with students (pilot CD screen grab: see previous page).*

Williams Each menu item marked with a plus sign has a submenu. So, for instance, there are several different sections of Fiona's masterclass to choose from in that submenu. You might, the first time that you use the CD-ROM, want to play through the entire masterclass section, but if you use it again or return to it for particular information, you could use the submenu as a bookmark, to lead you to the most relevant section of the class.

Goodman The 'Design' section includes notes on the various components of stage design – sets, props, lights, sound, costume, and the role and place of the audience – as well as on design concepts. Lee Livingstone, Light Designer at the University of Alberta, leads a masterclass on the basics of light. Her demonstrations are simple and yet extremely effective for multimedia teaching, since she shows how the colour spectrum breaks down under different lights.

The visual examples demonstrate the importance of choosing colours and fabrics for sets, props, and costumes which will work as sign systems on stage, and not be lost in the shift from one coloured or density light to another. Livingstone demonstrates the techniques of sculpting with light, and she points out that the choice of colour for costumes can make a huge difference to interpretation and performance: 'A designer can neutralize a character if she wants to; actors have to be friendly to designers.' Sample set models constructed for the heath scene in *Lear* are presented by their student designers, who explain their concepts and choices; the sets are then shown in close-up in white, blue, and red light.

Image 9 *Light Board (screen grab from pilot CD).*

Goodman All the design concepts from Module 2 are illustrated in Module 3, on 'Performance', with examples from three different director-designer teams' ways of imagining and creating the 'heath' from *King Lear* in the same black box set. Director Sandy Nichols worked with designer Jim Meers to create a metal junkyard, imported from a rubbish tip near Edmonton. They cast drama professor and professional actor Jim DeFelice as Lear, responding to the cues of Chris Dodd as Fool. Chris – a profoundly deaf actor who once had some hearing – makes an enormous racket with the metal 'heath', creating the soundscape of Storm over which Lear must shout to be heard.

Sign-language interpretation is available, though Chris's spoken language is perfectly clear, and the invented gestural language (an exaggerated sign language combined with familiar body-language techniques used to complement and underscore the delivery of the playtext) which this Lear and Fool

From the *Junkyard Lear*. Top: from the signed version. Bottom: Jim DeFelice as Lear (left) and Chris Dodd (himself profoundly deaf) as the Fool (right).

invented with Sandy Nichols is an effective form of communication in itself. Blue was the predominant colour in this interpretation, which has been described as Beckettian in visual and interpretive impact.

Image 10   *Junkyard Lear* (*above*).

In the second team's version, the director Beau Coleman worked with designer Brette Gerecke to create a multimedia performance concept for *Queen Lear:* Maralyn Ryan plays Lear, connected to a synthesizer making the music of Storm (conceived and performed by Darrin Hagen) on one side, and to a sampler making the soundscape of the Fool (performed by Dave Clarke) on the other.

The wires from these two machines are visibly attached to this Lear, as is the microphone at her mouth. The only light is that of a slide projector over the white muslin of her gown; the words of the play are, intermittently, projected onto the Queen.[5] White was the colour of this performance.

Image 11   *Queen Lear* (*see next page, left*).

Thirdly, the director Carl Hare worked with the designer David Lovett to create a mask-based interpretation of the same scene. Choosing to find the essential movements and gestures of the characters, this team spent time developing original masks which seem to communicate of their own accord. Emiko Kinoshita, a professional drummer with a Japanese troupe, portrays Storm, her drumsticks flying through the air making the sound of thunder and the look of lightning. John Kirkpatrick played Lear and Glen Gaston played Fool in this, the most text-sensitive interpretation of the three. The chosen colour gel for this version was red.

Image 12 *Masked Lear (above right, opposite).*

Coe These three very different approaches to the same scene threw up a number of logistical problems for recording. We clearly had to record this material in a different way from the *As You Like It* CD-ROM. Our three teams were given two days each to rehearse, and on the final day each in turn had an hour to set and light. They then performed their scene before an invited live audience, and we recorded it with two static cameras.

After the initial performance each group re-performed their scene three more times so the cameras could get different shots. In this way we ended up with eight complete recordings of the four performances. Then the next group moved into the space and the same thing happened all over again. This is a different technique to either normal out-of-sequence film/video shooting or multicamera recording a full theatrical performance. It enabled us not only to show what the audience could see but also to get in the action on stage and share that with distant audiences.

Goodman We recorded several speakers responding to these performances for the 'Experts' section on this CD-ROM, including Clive Barker (actor, director, teacher, and author of *Theatre Games*), Nicholas Barter (Principal, Royal Academy of Dramatic Arts), Julia Briggs (Professor of English at De Montfort University, and Shakespeare lecturer at Oxford), Graham Holderness (Professor of English at Watford University, Shakespeare scholar and editor), and Lisa Jardine (Professor of English at Queen Mary and Westfield College, University of London). Their feedback was recorded after they had seen all three alternative versions of the heath scene included on the CD-ROM.

They do not just discuss Shakespeare and performance in general terms; they critique and respond to the production extracts included on the CD-ROM. So part of the feedback loop is built in. The next part of that loop is activated when the users of the CD-ROM add their own views and ideas, typing them into the 'Notepad' and sharing them with colleagues, a tutor, or friends.

We recorded our experts in stages – the first two (Briggs and Holderness) at our own BBC studios in Milton Keynes, and the next three (Barter, Jardine, and Barker) at RADA. We fed the responses to our questions (critical and complimentary) into the digitiser and added them in a new 'Expert' section on the 'Help' task bar.

We then took the new CD-ROM for its official 'unveiling' at the World Shakespeare Congress in Los Angeles, and there we recorded dozens of interviews with scholars and practioners – Terence Hawkes, John Drakakis, Keir Elam, Catherine Belsey, Ania Loomba, Coppelia Kahn, Michael Bristol,

Opposite page, left: Darrin Hagen making the music of Storm as synthesizer in *Queen Lear*. Opposite page, right: Emiko Kinoshita as Storm in the *Masked Lear*. Above: The *Masked Lear*, with (left) John Kirkpatrick as Lear and (right) Glen Gaston as the Fool.

Jyotsna Singh, Jane Smiley, Christopher Ricks, Peter Donaldson, Reg Foakes, Stephen Greenblatt, Russ MacDonald, and many others – some for use on TV and video, and some for use on the CD-ROM.[6] Those on the CD-ROM included Kiernan Ryan, Terry Hawkes, Keir Elam, Reg Foakes, and Mary Hartman of Shakespeare and Co.

We recorded further interviews and feedback on the CD-ROMs throughout 1996, including the vox-pops for this MOMI lecture. All of this raw material is available to help us gauge responses to the multimedia Shakespeare experience, although we only include material for which we have attained formal rights through contract – so no one should find themselves included without consent.

Coe While disk capacity will not at present allow us to include more than a tiny fraction of all we've recorded, even a small amount sets the feedback loop in motion. When we showed the two CD-ROMs we received a great deal of very positive feedback, but even the most positive feedback leads to further revision – if you take others' views seriously. . . .

For about five minutes we were pretty pleased with ourselves, but then we moved into the next stage of feedback. Responses were positive, but they also offered some important points about what should still be added to the CD-ROM: responses which

seemed particularly appropriate considering that we were working in a university dedicated to the idea of giving people a second chance in education. And what did our feedback tell us was wanted? A different, more 'conventional' or 'traditional' version of that same storm scene.

Cue *soundbites of one expert after another saying that they'd like to see a 'more traditional' version of the scene, focusing more on the text . . . [three minutes].*

13. Back to the Drawing Board

[*Seven minutes*]

Goodman So we're back at work. Here's some new material we recorded earlier [in fact, only a week or so before the MOMI lecture was delivered]. Bravely agreeing to work with us yet again, Fiona Shaw took on the role of director of our selected scenes from *King Lear*. We gave her the feedback offered on the versions already included on the CD-ROM, and invited her to create her own interpretation which should, we asked, do something slightly more 'traditional' than the others . . . though of course none of us knew what might be meant by 'traditional'. We asked that the new version might focus more centrally on the text, leading to visual interpretations which arise naturally from the play.

Fiona took on this task and came back to us with a cast: Ken Cranham as Lear, Jude Akuwudike as Fool, Celia Imrie as Goneril, Lorraine Ashburn as Regan, and Aisling O'Sullivan as Cordelia. Fiona also offered us her idea of the set, the 'heath': a mental asylum. We searched for an asylum which would have us, as it were, somewhere near London, and settled on the disused psychiatric wing of Ealing General Hospital. They let us out a few hot summer days later with several new scenes from *Lear* and many new ideas. Tony took the tapes and set to work editing.

Coe   Hot off the editing bench, Fiona's re-working of the declaration scene.

Image 13   *Ealing Lear (see following page).*

Coe   Our aim here, as always, was to try and find a way of providing our audience with a performance with some contemporary resonance, something that they could connect to. We wanted to concentrate attention on the words and the language. Our next project is to refine and develop this material into a fully functional interactive CD-ROM – one of the new CDs in the series in progress.[7]

14. End Credits

[*Two minutes*]

Cue   *light on podium.*

Goodman   Everything we have shared so far is still very much work in progress, but we hope that it has demonstrated some of the possibilities for using new technology to enhance the study of theatre, Shakespeare, and culture more generally. The feedback loop of any learning process is continuous. We've built in a number of feedback loops for users of the CD-ROMs, including 'Note-pads' and links to the World Wide Web which lead to a number of the most exciting Shakespeare sites around the world, thereby creating an even larger 'virtual classroom', or 'virtual world theatre'.

Now we'll be collecting more feedback, to begin the next phase of working backwards: so in a moment we'll turn back over to you, but for now, let's hear what one of today's leading theatre directors has to say.

Cue   *end credits.*

Shakespeare Plugged and Unplugged
the Lecture
was brought to you by
THE OPEN UNIVERSITY BBC
SHAKESPEARE MULTIMEDIA RESEARCH PROJECT

Interactive CD-ROMs
written and presented by
LIZBETH GOODMAN

Produced by
TONY COE

Programmed by
HUW WILLIAMS
with
NATHANIEL CROSS AND CHARON WOOD

Artistic Associate
FIONA SHAW

Camera-operators on location in Canada
DARON DONOHUE, RANDY TOMIAK

Sound
PATRICK TRONCHON

Student Video Diarists
JANET MAH, GARY BLANEY, JENNIFER MCCAFFREY

Production Manager
DALE PHILLIPS
with assistance from
JAYNE ELLERY, JILL TIBBLE

Interactive Web Site by
STEPHEN REGAN AND STEPHEN REIMER

This Lecture Presentation
was written by
LIZBETH GOODMAN
with
TONY COE AND HUW WILLIAMS
with 'unplugged' performances by
NEIL D'SOUZA AND CLARE BLOOMER OF RADA

Produced by
CHRIS PALMER AND TONY COE

with production assistance from
JULIE ACKROYD
and with vox-pop contributions by
THE ASSEMBLED COMPANY

From the 'Ealing *Lear*'. Top: Jude Akuwudike as the Fool (left) and Celia Imrie as Goneril (right).
Bottom: Fiona Shaw (left) in rehearsal in the disused psychiatric wing of Ealing General Hospital,
with Kenneth Cranham as Lear and Celia Imrie as Goneril.

Peter Sellars Two hundred years ago is just too long for anyone to know how it's supposed to go. So if they try to tell you, don't listen! How would they know? *How would they know? (Laughter.)*

Cue *flash the words – 'Exeunt, Logout'.*

Fade to black. Slowly fade up house lights.

Actors' curtain call. Actors takes seats in audience. The Open University's Vice Chancellor, Sir John Daniel, joins us on the stage to say a few words and chair the question session.[8]

Notes and References

1. The *As You Like It* video was produced by Amanda Willett for the Open University/BBC in 1994, and was first used by some 3,800 OU students on the 'Approaching Literature' course in 1995. The video features Fiona Shaw working with students from LAMDA, extracts from the Cheek by Jowl all-male production, and a new version of the Banishment scene directed by Fiona Shaw, with Susan Lynch and Matilda Zeigler, in the disused St. Pancras Chambers, London. The video also includes interviews with Shaw, Deborah Warner, Annie Castledine, Declan Donnellan, and Peter Sellars. It is available from Routledge as part of the 'Approaching Literature' multimedia series. Extracts from the video were included in the TV programme 'Girls Who Are Boys' (presented by Fiona Shaw; academic associate Lizbeth Goodman; produced by Tony Coe), the third in the new showcase series, *Conjuring Shakespeare*, broadcast on BBC2 at 7.30 pm for six weeks in September–October 1997 . The video and a range of other multimedia materials are discussed in the book *Shakespeare, Aphra Behn, and the Canon*, eds. W. R. Owens and L. Goodman (Routledge, 1996).

2. The question 'how can we use technology before it uses us?' was posed as one of the throughlines to a conference/performance festival, 'Gender in the Field of Vision', held at the Gate Theatre, London, on 5 July 1997 (hosted by the OU/BBC Gender in Writing and Performance Research Group, with speakers and performers including Leslie Hill, Helen Paris, Peter Ride, Huw Williams, Susan Kozel, Janet Adshead-Lansdale, Mara de Wit, Kim Morrissey, Katharine Cockin, Dorothea Smartt, Patience Agbabi, Adeola Agbebiyi and Joan Lipkin (in a 'virtual keynote' delivered by choral performance from the floor of a script posted in advance); chaired by Lizbeth Goodman and organized by Jane de Gay, with assistance from the ACE Combined Arts Unit. Responses to this question were discussed as part of the plenary discussion following each session and were also recorded on video by Carli Leimbach of Headlong Productions. Videos can be ordered c/o Jane de Gay, Department of Literature, Arts Faculty, Open University, Walton Hall, Milton Keynes MK7 6AA, or via the 'Gender in Writing and Performance' web site (address below).

3. *King Lear in Performance* pilot CD-ROM, prototype version, first presented at the World Shakespeare Congress, Los Angeles, 7-14 April, 1996. Written and presented by Lizbeth Goodman; designed and programmed by Huw Williams, Charon Wood, and Nathaniel Cross; produced by Tony Coe. Featuring a master class with Fiona Shaw (Artistic Associate). Web site created by Stephen Regan and Stephen Reimer. CD-ROM produced by the Open University Faculty of Arts and BBC, with BBC Interactive Media; supported by a grant from the Office of Technology Development. Produced in collaboration with the University of Alberta, Routledge (publishers of the latest Arden edition, as yet unpublished text kindly provided by Reg Foakes), and the Royal Academy of Dramatic Arts.

4. In 1995, the Shakespeare Multimedia Research Project won an award which funded a formal study of these two CD-ROMs by Jan Rae and Ellie Chambers of the Institute of Educational Technology. That research is ongoing, and the results are feeding into the revision of the CD-ROMs for international release. The CD-ROMs and the video materials which they incorporate will be used on the new Open University 'Shakespeare: Text and Performance' course, to be first presented to students in the year 2000.

5. Teresa Dobson from the University of Alberta has written an original critique of the *Queen Lear* design concept and performance, for publication in a future issue of *New Theatre Quarterly*.

6. Interviews conducted by Stephen Regan, Lizbeth Goodman, and Bob Owens, produced by Jenny Bardwell, assisted by Jayne Ellery, for the Open University BBC at the World Shakespeare Congress, Los Angeles, April 1996.

7. The three storm scenes are included and discussed in the 'Stormy Weather' programme (No. 4), and the 'Ealing Lear' scenes are included in the 'It's a Family Affair' programme (No. 5) in the new showcase TV series, *Conjuring Shakespeare*, broadcast on BBC2 at 7.30 pm for six weeks in September–October 1997. 'Stormy Weather' was narrated by Fiona Shaw and produced by Jenny Bardwell. 'It's a Family Affair' was narrated by Lizbeth Goodman and produced by Tony Coe. For full details on programmes, write to the Open University Showcase TV Series, OU/BBC Production Centre, Walton Hall, Milton Keynes MK7 6BH, or via the Shakespeare Multimedia Project web site (address below).

8. A related paper investigating the uses of media in teaching about performance has been written and delivered by Lizbeth Goodman at the Oxford CTI conference on Media-Assisted Learning, St. Anne's College, Oxford, 17 March 1997. That lecture was videoed, and has been published as 'Creative Imagination and Media-Assisted Learning: Shakespeare in Performance', in *The Journal of Literary and Linguistic Computing*, November 1997.

For Further Information

See the Web site: http://www.Open.ac.uk/OU/Academic/Arts/Shakespr.htm *and the related Web site:* http://www.Open.ac.uk/OU/Academic/Arts/Literature/Gender/gender.htm

Leslie Hill

'Push the Boat Out': Site-Specific and Cyberspatial in Live Art

As a mutually-illuminating contrast to the academic exploration in the previous article of the potential of CD-ROM as a means both of teaching a 'classical' playtext and of analyzing the multiple choices involved in its performance, the two following pieces explore the potential of the new technologies in the creation and documentation of live art. Focusing upon her performance *Push the Boat Out*, given as part of the Jezebel Season at the Institute of Contemporary Arts in 1995, Leslie Hill first outlines the thinking behind her use of the Internet and the Web – as yet more economic than CD-ROM – both for creating 'live art' and for rendering its conventionally 'unprintable' form as a 'text' with its own integrity. The scripted element of her performance follows. Leslie Hill is a writer and performer, currently a resident artist fellow at the Institute for Studies in the Arts, and a senior lecturer in the Theatre Department at Arizona State University. Along with Helen Paris, she is co-artistic director of the 'curious.com' multimedia performance company.

THE FOLLOWING is an account of how a weekend I spent on a boat on a lake in Oklahoma in 1994 became a weekend I spent on a boat in a time-based installation at the ICA in 1995 became a voyage into cyberspace in 1996 – the metamorphosis from 'real' to performance to virtual.

A little self-conscious of the title of this article, I confess that my work in the past has not been site-specific in the sense that I have created performances for public toilets, bowling alleys, or National Trust properties. My usage of the term here is perhaps inappropriate in its evocation of an *oeuvre* to which my work does not technically belong, so before going any further let me qualify.

I use the term 'site-specific' in this article for several reasons. Firstly, I have never transferred a performance from one venue to another without radically altering it in relation to the institution, the season, or the performance space, so in this sense my performance work has been venue and programme specific. Secondly, I regard showing work at the ICA, to give an institutional example, to be at least as contextually complex and inherently circumscribed by cultural and critical referents as showing work in a pasture or a laundrette, and

therefore regard work made for the ICA to be site-specific.

Thirdly, if I go to the trouble of creating a time-based installation as the setting for my performance, I should be allowed to call the performance site-specific. Fourth, the spatial and temporal emphemerality of live work predisposes me to regard a large proportion of it as site-specific – reminiscent of Walter Benjamin's definition of the traditional contextualization of art as occurring within the 'cult' situation of a unique moment of contact between the art and the audience at a specific place and time.

Fifthly, the shifting relationship between place and 'placelessness' brought about by the rapid adoption of the Internet as a preferred form of communication leads me, at times, to regard all real-space, real-time events as site-specific as opposed to 'cyberspatial' works – their reception occurring in the largely intangible interface between the human mind and the computer. As my interest here is primarily in the move from 'site-specific' performance and installation into such computer-formatted work, I shall spare the details of my 'real life' weekend on the boat in Oklahoma and skip straight to the yellow rubber raft in the ICA theatre.[1]

43

Site-Specific

In *Push the Boat Out* I constructed an American landscape of ignorance, greed, and discontent, a territory where the rich get meaner, the poor get trashier, and no one expects to keep their own teeth past the age of thirty-five. At the base of this installation was a giant map of the USA made from photocopy enlargements of (then) current tabloid newspapers: OKLAHOMA CITY BOMBER IS MAN OF MY DREAMS; THREE SEMI-AUTOMATICS FOR FUN!; O.J.'S ANGUISH – NICOLE WAS A LESBIAN. . . .

I covered the map in a thick, rank rennet of consumables from the trashy white underbelly of America: Moonpies, Twinkies, Runts, Nerds, Bubble Brains, Beef Jerky, Licorice Super Ropes, Pocahontas Sweet-tarts, Power Rangers Fruit Chews, etc. A film screen above the map featured American TV clips from July 1995: the Praise the Lord Club; QVC cable shopping; Days of Our Lives; WWF Wrestling; the Psychic Hotline; confessional talk shows; O. J. Simpson's trial; and the gala Fourth of July celebrations at the White House.

From a yellow rubber raft positioned in the centre of the map, I generated a counter discourse. Floating in the sea of trash consumables were various messages in bottles which I tape-recorded and placed (in personal stereos) inside 64-ounce 'Big Gulp' drinks containers. I sent out hundreds of narrative fragments *via* text confetti, paper airplanes, and red, white, and blue helium balloons which acted as carrier pigeons. These texts were stories, recipes, statements, and questions generated in response to trash culture. A video camera, twenty disposable cameras, tape recorders, and blank post-cards were littered about, with which the audience were invited to document their impressions and experiences.

I defined the border between 'America' and the ICA floor (Britain) with a six-inch high, six-inch thick line of pure refined salt and sugar, which followed the contours of the map. Over the two-day period, as patrons waded back and forth steadily consuming the map, the border blurred beyond recognition. Occasionally, anxious Brits attempted to sweep it back into place, saying, 'But you can't tell it's *America* any more.' I looked around at all those empty cans and empty wrappers and thought: *my point exactly.*

Still in my raft by night, I gave a one-hour monologue each evening to a conventionally seated theatre audience, succinctly perfor-ming some of the text which had been drifting piecemeal through the installation. The differences in reception between the spoken text and the written text were fas-cinating to me as a writer/performer. Both texts consisted of the same words, distri-buted by the same person from the same boat, pitted against the same elements in the same art space, but were accorded very different status.

The spoken text, which demanded no direct interaction on the part of the audi-ence, was accorded higher rank from the outset (partly by virtue of the fact that admission to the performance cost five pounds more than admission to the instal-lation). The printed text – language intended for consumption when I carefully folded it into paper airplanes – seemed to become 'garbage' the moment it hit the floor, an im-passe from which only the audience could rescue it.

The spoken text, in contrast, was instantly given the audience's full and uninterrupted attention. The difficulty, from my perspec-tive as a would-be communicator, was that during the installation the audience clicked into the 'trash' discourse of TV clips and Twinkies with such ease, such relish, that most of my text seemed to be hopelessly swamped.

The fear of this rather desperate dynamic is what fuelled the piece in the first place, so I can't say I was surprised that the people who came to the installation seemed to ingest more of the trash than the text – that the trash is what they put into their bodies and took home with them – but I hadn't counted on the emotional impact this would have on me as the person struggling to communicate through the mire. As the hours went by and I knew that the map of America was slowly seeping through the bodies of patrons and into the sewage system of greater London, I wondered if anyone had taken a piece of my text home in their pockets.

Whereas the installation made me feel isolated and dispirited as a would-be communicator, the first evening performance brought me back into a reassuring feeling of direct contact with the audience. When I conceptualized the piece I never anticipated the personal difficulties I would have with the silent performances within the installation. Why, I wondered, was sitting amidst my installation distributing text so uncomfortable? As a writer I was accustomed to representing myself through printed texts, albeit I didn't normally have to be in the room with people while they read them. As a performer, I realized that I was used to controlling the space and the audience during performances.

In previous works the audience was very specifically controlled in terms of what they could see, what they could hear, which space they occupied, how they entered, how they exited, etc. In creating a highly interactive installation, I had relinquished a great deal of this control. If audience members chose to eat twelve feet of Licorice Super Rope while watching Jan Crouch spin the globe for Jesus on the Trinity Broadcast Network and never engage with my presence, my messages in bottles, or my text, that was entirely their prerogative.

I had to remind myself, however, of the perverse pleasure I had taken in amassing the 'Wurmz'n'Dirt' and Pocahontas candies; the sinful hours I had spent snorting and chortling as I edited TV clips of demonically possessed soap opera characters; and my guilty obsession with the *Women and Guns* magazines. I had to shake myself out of the feeling that my work was being ignored by an audience who actually preferred neon orange peanut butter and cheese crackers and WWF Lumberjack Wrestling to my narratives, and realize that the audience, most likely, shared my horrified fascination with full-frontal trash culture. Of course a

normal person was bound to engage with a giant film screen and a ton of Moonpies before they got round to unfolding paper airplanes.

Their consumption, however, like my own, was not callow or uncritical. By the second day I had relaxed into my role in the installation and begun to enjoy my eagle's nest view of the interaction between audience, trash, text, and performance. I became much less competitive about how my own texts were faring in relation to the trash, and much more critically interested in people's patterns of consumption.

Cyberspatial

My initial interest in multimedia computer work came as a direct result of my quandary as to how best to document *Push the Boat Out*. The elements, of course, were all thematically interrelated, but the structure was non-linear and the form ranged from film and television to home-movies to beer-can sculpture to postcards to tape recordings to text to live performance to footprints in the detritus.

Not only was I faced with the problem of documenting the trash components of the installation and my own text and performance, but also with over two hundred photographs and four hours of video taken by audience members, as well as their postcard responses and the patterns with which they had consumed and redistributed trash and text. Obviously, the performance text and video came nowhere near standing as an adequate representation of the project.

Around the same time, I began using the Internet, and the *modus operandus* of jumping from a hypertext hot link to a photograph, video clip, or sound bite and from one Web site to another instantly appealed to me. In a book format one faces the necessity of arranging narrative in a linear fashion – no matter how experimental the form or content, the author still commits to a page 1, 2, 3 sequence. In hypertext, however, I could arrange the different pieces of 'trash', personal and audience narratives, and images in a series of links unlimited in their complexity, a format much more akin to the installation itself, where sequence and interrelation were dependent on the enfranchisement of the perceiver.

Of course, navigating through a series of electronic links could never recreate the atmospheric qualities of the installation – moving one at a time from one screen field to another bears little relation to the experience of standing in a ton of trash reading a story plucked from a passing helium balloon while fireworks explode over the White House on the film screen above your head and someone snaps a Polaroid picture of you spitting Pepperoni Pizza-flavoured Corn Nuts. For the more visceral aspects of live art, technology will always be hard pressed to eliminate the adage, 'You really had to be there.'

For me, the point was not whether one could recreate, through technology, an installation environment, but simply that technology offered some very exciting new options in the notoriously difficult project of live art documentation. Formally a *Push the Boat Out* hypertext could never resemble the live work, but conceptually a series of text, image, sound, and video links navigated by individual readers/viewers/users seemed closer in spirit than a set text or straight video could ever be.

The primary choice, as I saw it, for the artist interested in developing computer formatted work was between Web publishing and CD-ROM. As a live artist, the 'live' nature of the Internet held obvious appeal – being 'on-line' is a live situation in a way that reading a book or watching a film is not, because in exploring the Internet you are downloading images and information from the source in the moment – i.e., as you navigate. The live aspect of the Internet makes it ideal for time-based work: sites can be updated weekly, hourly, or every few seconds not only by the artist but by the people who visit the site.

The Internet Appeal

On World AIDS Day 1996, for example, the ArtAIDS Web site launched Nick Crowe's *One Day and All of the Night*, an Internet performance of sunrises, sunsets, and lovers over twenty-four hours around the world. On another branch of the ArtAIDS site, Zara Waldeback, Lois Weaver, and myself designed a Lost and Found department where visitors were invited, over a one-year period, to submit images and stories of things, people, and feelings lost and found. In the first instance the viewer would download a specific moment of an ever-changing site, in the second instance the visitor could become a co-creator of an ever-growing site. Both situations are dynamic/time-based.

The second major attraction of the Web was that on a Web site the artist could design internal links between visual and textual elements of their own work, as well as external links to other relevant sites on the Web such as Anglicans Online!, the Captain James T. Kirk Sing-a-Long page, Cyberstars, or the Interactive Frog Dissection site. In this way, work could branch out and interconnect in uniquely interesting, contemporary ways.

The last, but certainly not least great draw of the Internet as far as I was concerned was and is its relatively inexpensive nature, which allows people such as myself who are making work from the margins to self-publish.

CD-ROM holds quite a different appeal, the most important being superior quality and speed. As a performer, I have been accustomed to cutting and pasting freely from photography, music, video, etc. – a practice which is severely limited, as yet, on the Internet. A photograph or some simple animation can take several minutes to download from the Net, and video and audio can take a small eternity with infuriatingly poor results.

While I accept that a certain amount of download time is inevitable, as a performer I would never leave an audience sitting in boredom for five minutes at frequent intervals during a show and expect them to stick around. If the Web is to be capitalized on as an alternative performance space, this must be done with the abilities and limitations of the 'venue' in mind: therefore, while sophisticated networks of internal and external links and interactive time-based projects are ideal for the Web, audio and video and animation work is much better left to CD-ROM.[2]

While a CD-ROM doesn't have the 'live' or time-based quality of a Web site, it offers a much greater formal range to the artist, as well as having the classic integrity of a 'finished' or complete piece of work. Because *Push the Boat Out* consisted of and generated so many photographs, video and audio clips, CD-ROM would obviously have been the more suitable format for expanding this piece into an electronic work. Sadly, the average cost of developing a CD-ROM in 1996 was around $30,000, which in live art terms is pricey.

Push the Boat Out was never developed into a CD-ROM, but it did lead me to a great interest in the potentials of electronic venues, potentials which I am currently exploring and exploiting in new works designed specifically for computer technology.

As a performer, making work for the Internet or a CD-ROM will never induce the adrenaline rush of a live performance, but neither, I suspect, would it generate feelings of the isolation and alienation I described as part of my experience in a durational performance. In 1994 I found a message in a bottle on the beach on Arran Island off the west coast of Scotland: it was scrawled in pencil and decorated with Jelly Babies. In 1995 I scattered tape-recorded messages in bottles throughout my performance installation. In 1996 I posted my first hypertext, *Deus ex Machina*, onto the Internet in much the same spirit as one might cast a bottle upon the waves.

One can, of course, classify these different forms of communication as 'real', 'performance', and 'virtual', or as examples of place and placelessness or site-specific and cyber-spatial experience; but the salient point, as far as I'm concerned, is that the common denominator of both sending and receiving still resides in living, breathing human bodies.

Notes

1. I felt it was important to mention that the performance and installation stemmed from a real-life event not because I am interested (here) in tracing the evolution of personal experience to public art, but rather from a philosophical interest in notions of place and placelessness. I note the 'real' boat in Oklahoma, then, in so much as it was the site of a 'site-specific' experience.

2. Laurie Anderson's *Puppet Motel* (1994) is, as yet, by far and away the best performance work I've seen on CD-ROM and I recomend anyone who hasn't had the pleasure of exploring it to buy or borrow a copy in the next twenty-four hours.

Leslie Hill

Deus ex Machina: Navigating between the Lines

GOOD EVENING. Tonight I've been asked to talk to you about HTML – hypertext markup language – and its performative characteristics; its multimedia capacity; its non-linear structure; its interactive possibilities; its real-time relationship with its readers slash navigators slash audience; and its potential interest to writers cum artists cum performers.

My lovely assistant this evening is Zara Waldeback, who will be navigating through a sea of text, context, hypertext, subtext, classical texts, and poached texts. What you see behind me is a live video projection of Zara's computer screen and her own personal navigation choices. Now all this and more is attached to the ICA website, so please feel free to try this at home later. For those of you who aren't on line, you'll find some of this text strewn about your seats, so please feel equally free to take this home and pleasure yourselves with it.

Anyway, for starters, I'd like to talk about my holiday to Greece. I'll tell you up front that I sold my computer to finance this holiday, which may or may not have some relevance to my relationship with technology. I had recently watched the breathtaking spectacle of Michel Foucault morphing into a Power Ranger on an American university professor's website and I wanted to learn more about this type of fluid relationship, and so the ancient Greeks had been on my mind.

Their interactive, multimedia relationship with their gods interested me and I was keen to visit the landscape where these remarkable morphings from god to human to animal to monster had actually taken place. Throughout history, myth and religion have been site-specific affairs, and so it was obvious that I would need to make the trip in person, and my penchant for feta cheese and stuffed vine-leaves only strengthened this conviction. This is how the chair in front of my computer morphed into a seat on a charter flight.

Now, Greek mythology as we know it starts with Zeus's overthrow of his father, Cronus the child-eater, and because of this I decided that my pilgrimage should be to the Idean cave, Mount Ida, Crete, the actual geographic location of the birthplace of Zeus. I had spent the spring fretting about Baudrillard's simulacra and the desert of the real and it seemed, at the time, that a visit to the Idean cave would help.

Note: that the simulacra, according to Baudrillard, is a truth which conceals a non-existence – for example: the icons which conceal the absence of God; the Disneyland theme park, which exists in order to make the rest of Los Angeles appear real; or Watergate, which triumphed in promoting the idea that it actually *was* a scandal in American politics.[1]

The Greek gods are dead now, of course, which is a shame. Zeus, whose name means 'bright one', ruled the universe by the power of the thunderbolt and would, I think, have been particularly at home in the electronic age. Then again, it might just have pissed him off – humans harnessing his medium so skilfully. Remember what he did to Prometheus for giving us a simple flame in a fennel-stalk. The creation of the World Wide Web could really have had livers flying if Zeus were still around. And let's not forget that Prometheus wasn't the only one who got punished for the exchange of fire. Zeus punished man in another way by creating an evil thing, according to the mythographers, the biggest single bad thing Zeus ever made, yes: WOMAN.

Aside: girls, they're casting us as the instrument of the devil again and, as they say, where there's smoke there's fire, and Woman, after all, is the price of fire. So when you use your personal computers, girls, remember Pandora's box and THINK BIG.

Anyway, during the spring, I had been thinking about Walter Benjamin and his observation that the contextual integration of art in tradition found its expression in the cult, and that 'even the most perfect reproduction of a work of art is lacking in one element: its presence in time and space, its unique existence in the place where it happens to be.'[2]

Because I was working, at the time, on a hypertext narrative for the Web, I got to wondering about art which exists only within cyberspace. Is it an original which has transcended the need for reproduction or it is a simulation that supersedes the need for the existence of an 'authentic' original? Is cyberspace site-specific or is cyberspace a realm of placelessness?

You see, as a live artist, I never felt that Benjamin's essay, 'The Work of Art in the Age of Mechanical Reproduction', particularly applied to me, and the fact that I present my text in the flesh seemed, to me, to refute Baudrillard's desert of the real.

Note: Borges tells a fable of an emperor who commissions a map of his empire so splendid, so accurate, that it covers the territory like a second skin. As the empire declines, the map begins to rot and disintegrate until the only vestiges which survive are dry, charred parchments littering the desert. According to Baudrillard, the fable has been reversed and, in the age of electronic simulation, it is the 'real', the territory, which we now find rotting against the fabric of the hyperreal, the map.[3]

In creating an electronic work, I wondered, was I inadvertently supporting Baudrillard's theory that abstraction today is the generation by models of a real without origin or reality – a hyperreal? Was I, a live artist, batting for the wrong team? Bolstering the idea that the territory no longer precedes the map, nor survives it? That the hype . . . rrrrr precedes the text?

Anyway, the road to Mount Ida was treacherous. I was driving all day in the blazing sun and my brakes were overheating from going round so many hairpin curves. I jostled along a dirt track until I came to an enormous car park full of schoolchildren shouting. Although there were a hell of a lot of people in the car park, the path up the mountain appeared to be deserted. The higher I climbed, the more I could see of the green bowl-shaped valley below and the less I could see of the mountain itself.

Eventually I came over a rise and there was a small white church, a graveyard, a tree, and, strangely, an abandoned miniature railway track. From here the path became narrower and rockier and little by little the upper lip of the cave came into view. I noticed a man in a Yankees baseball cap sitting under a tree, watching me. I carried on to the mouth of the cave and I stood there staring into the mossy darkness. Then

I noticed that there was a strange wire fence barring the entrance to the cave. It had a gate, but the gate was locked. The man in the Yankees cap appeared noiselessly from behind and produced the key.

I walked down into the cave where the air was cold and still, and stood there listening to the water dripping down the walls, looking up at the gatekeeper's silhouette against the blue sky. I was wondering about what sort of size the infant Zeus might have been. The cave was big, but it wasn't colossal, and it got me to thinking about the futurists and how their key prediction for the twenty-first century is 'placelessness': the idea that fibre-optic communications networks will be the place to be, so that we are everywhere and nowhere, baby; the idea that information which was expressed, contained and exchanged in atoms will be translated to bits, to electronic signals; that the attaché case handcuffed to the wrist of the secret agent will become a blip down a phone line.

An idea I was particularly interested in was Marsall McLuhan's theory that, unlike the interactive Greek gods, who indulged in plenty of intercourse – some of it divine, some otherwise – the Christian God has suffered acute loneliness since the creation of the universe, having no one to communicate with on his own level. And this Roman Catholic philosopher believes that it has always been the project of humankind to create a collective consciousness capable of bridging this gap. In the Internet, a communications network born of an abandoned military intelligence system, he thinks we are achieving our destiny.[4] If humans are the brain cells and fibre optics are the neurons, could it be that the planet is waking up – that the planet is becoming sentient? Hey nonny.

Note: Prometheus had taken great pains to imprison all the spites that might plague the human race in a jar which he warned his brother Epimetheus to keep sealed. But Epimetheus's beautiful, mischievous wife (wouldn't you know), Pandora, opened the jar releasing a cloud of stinging chaos. This is how humankind came to be tormented with, among other things, Hope.

Anyway, what I had absolutely no way of knowing was that throughout my pilgrimage, I was incubating something. Something that had imperceptibly made its way into my body and was about to completely alter my topography. The first sign I noticed was a clear blister the size of a split pea on my inner thigh. And then there was one on my back and then there was one behind my ear. By the time my flight landed at Gatwick my back and shoulders were erupting in these clear blisters and I was starting to get kinda itchy. Twenty-four hours later, my torso had morphed into a mass of hundreds of swollen red itching vesicles full to bursting with the foul herpied fluids of chicken pox.

As one crop of vesicles matured to murky yellow pustules, oozing at the centre, fresh crops of macules and papules were erupting on my arms and legs and face and scalp, in my ears, in my nose, in my mouth, on my tongue, on my eyelids, around my anus, and on my clitoris. I was a sinner in the hands of an angry virus. I became sweaty and feverish and I lay awake three nights in a row, my torso on fire, my nerve endings flayed, my limbs twitching.

As the sores thickened into farinaceous, phlegmy boils it became difficult and painful to peel myself from the crusty sheets. I looked out the second-storey window and wondered if leaping out would be an act extreme enough to counteract what was happening to me. Eventually I scabbed over. Everyone said – don't pick them off or you'll be permanently scarred. And I asked myself, which would you rather have: scars for life, or these scabs on your body one more minute? I picked a hundred scabs off my torso and hoovered the carpet.

The whole experience put me in mind of a little poem by the body-loathing, techno-worshipping David Skal:

– mindbody meatbody deathbody stinking sagging shitting fetus bursting organs hanging buried alive in a coffin of blood oh god not me don't let it be me got to get out of this bucket of tripe it's sucking me down throwing me up take it away this pulsing writhing spurting spinning body-go-round, BODY –[5]

Normally I don't have a lot of time for this sort of post-human, transcendental Nietzschean Modern Body Meat Hell stuff. I mean, I have absolutely no interest in downloading my spirit into a machine: if it can't feel pleasure and pain, I'm not interested. I think the whole post-human escape velocity theory, the theory that we can escape from our bodies and our mortality in the same way that a space ship can escape the gravitational pull of the earth, is a load of bollocks, to use a site-specific metaphor. I will admit, however, that the pox added a whole new dimension to my understanding of what it means to occupy a human body, but I'll live with the scars. It's one way of maintaining the reality/signifier distinction.

You know, the phrase 'the medium is the message' puts me in mind of the Delphic oracle: all it's messages were offal. But seriously, if the medium is the message, I wonder how we as writers are meant to communicate in a world where our texts become obsolete before we can finish writing them? I mean, if Homer was creating *The Iliad* today as a multimedia hypertext narrative, the technology would have changed long before he finished it, so there is something to be said for the comparative stability of the printed word, of atomic text.

But electronic text is intoxicating, as Richard Lanham elucidates:

Hot type was set. Digital typesetting programs pour or flow. Hypertexts are, in more than a manner of speaking, three-dimensional. Fugue-like, they carry several levels simultaneously. We talk a lot about 'subtexts' and such, but what if several are actually there in residence? Again, electronic text literalizes a theoretical conundrum. No 'final cut' means no conventional endings, or beginnings or middles either. All of this yields a body of work active not passive, a canon not frozen in perfection but volatile with contending human motive.[6]

Note: *deus ex machina* literally translates as: god from the machine. The expression is used to denote an unlikely agent which arrives to resolve an apparently hopeless situation; or, a contrived and inartistic solution of a difficulty in plot.

Being a humanist as well as a generally optimistic person, I tend to reject nihilism whenever possible, so the desert of the real holds little attraction for me. Instead, I agree with Laurie Anderson that technology is simply the campfire around which we now tell our stories. The origin and audience are still in living, breathing human bodies.

Thank you. Goodnight.

Notes and References

1. Jean Baudrillard, *Simulations* (New York: Semiotext[e], 1983), p. 1, 8, 25, 27.
2. Walter Benjamin, 'Art in the Age of Mechanical Reproduction', in *Illuminations*, ed. Hannah Arendt (New York: Schocken Books, 1985), p. 220.
3. Jean Baudrillard, *Simulations*, p. 1-4.
4. Mark Dery, *Escape Velocity*.
5. Ibid.
6. Richard A. Lanham, *The Electronic Word: Democracy, Technology, and the Arts* (Chicago: University of Chicago Press, 1993), p. 21.

Rudolf Weiss

Harley Granville Barker:
the First English Chekhovian?

Harley Granville Barker, the major innovator in the English theatre at the beginning of the present century, was long underestimated as a playwright, and misjudged as a mediocre imitator of Bernard Shaw. In more recent years major revivals of his plays, as well as new critical studies and editions, have witnessed a renewed interest in Barker as a dramatist, which, Rudolf Weiss here argues, testifies to the Chekhovian rather than the Shavian qualities of his plays. In the following article Weiss explores these qualities in the context of the early reception of Chekhov's plays in Britain, and on the basis of a reassessment of the existing records he offers a new view of Barker's originality as a playwright, concluding that the quasi-Chekhovian stamp of his work does not derive from influence but reflects the distinctive *zeitgeist* of the turn of the twentieth century. Rudolf Weiss, who teaches in the English Department of the University of Vienna, has previously published on Arthur Wing Pinero, John Galsworthy, Harley Granville Barker, and Elizabeth Baker.

GEORGE BERNARD SHAW used to compare his own plays to the music of Giuseppe Verdi and Barker's to the music of Claude Debussy. The French composer has often been labelled as an Impressionist, as was the Russian writer Anton Chekhov. Sam Walters, who directed the world premieres of Barker's last two plays – *The Secret Life* at the Orange Tree Theatre, Richmond, in 1988 and *His Majesty* for the Edinburgh Festival in 1992 – points out the distinction between Shaw's and Barker's plays, and the similarities between Barker and Chekhov:

In England we, of course, have this link with Shaw, and tend to think that Granville Barker is some sort of paperback version of Shaw, and he's not. He's a totally different sort of playwright. He's much more like Chekhov. It's much more a matter of having to discover what's going on in the scenes, what the subtext is.[1]

The present paper will not venture to place Barker's dramatic *oeuvre* in the context of Impressionism, to cast him as a Debussy of English drama, but to explore his affinity with Chekhov.

The stereotype of the reception history of Barker's plays, which holds them second-rate epigonic Shaw, has recently been revised. In *Harley Granville Barker: an Edinburgh Retro-*spective 1992, a record of the Barker season at the Edinburgh International Festival, many of the contributing scholars, critics, and directors define Barker's dramatic technique in terms of its likeness to that of the Russian master. Indeed, in Barker criticism *Chekhovian*, as a complimentary epithet, with its connotation of originality and subtextual complexity, has replaced the time-worn, unflattering *Shavian*, with its implication of mere imitation. But what has been lacking is an exploration of the relationship between Chekhov and Barker on the basis of the early reception of Chekhov in Britain and a comparative analysis of key features of their plays.

Harley Granville Barker developed his dramatic technique in the final years of the nineteenth and the first years of the twentieth century,[2] at a time before Chekhov's plays had first appeared in print in English translations[3] or had been first produced in British theatres.[4] It is highly unlikely that Barker knew any unpublished translations at this early stage, and whether he became acquainted with Chekhov's plays in English in the following few years remains a moot point.

News of the Chekhov productions at the Moscow Art Theatre had attracted the attention of the theatrical avant-garde. In 1905 Bernard Shaw, whose work for the theatre is of an entirely different mould but who came to admire Chekhov's plays, expressed an interest in a Russian author whose name he was not quite sure of remembering correctly. In a letter to Laurence Irving of 25 October 1905 he inquires about available translations:

I hear that there are several dramas extant by Whatshisname (Tchekoff, or something like that). . . . Have you any of them translated for the Stage Society, or anything of your own that would suit us? We are in a hole for the moment, as all the plays we used to get now go to Vedrenne [and] Barker.[5]

However, the next we hear from Shaw on Chekhov and the British stage is his complaint about the reception of and audience behaviour at the Stage Society performance of *The Cherry Orchard* in 1911: 'An exquisite play by Tchekoff was actually hissed. You cannot conceive how inferior we are (a small circle excepted) to the common playgoer.'[6]

Problems of Early Chekhov Reception

There is some evidence that St. John Hankin, a new dramatist whose major plays were all first performed either by the Stage Society (an institution which he also served as a member of the Council of Management) or at the Court Theatre as part of the highly acclaimed Barker/Vedrenne repertory experiment, championed Chekhov. In 1907, in a review of two now-forgotten plays by other authors, Hankin introduces Chekhov as the guiding spirit of what he regards as a new dramatic movement:

Persons who have followed the movements of the contemporary stage on the Continent with any attention know that one of its most interesting developments of recent years has been the rise of the Moscow school of drama of which Tchekoff is the prophet.[7]

Subsequently, Hankin elaborates on Chekhov's dramatic technique yet without referring to individual dramas. Nevertheless, his analysis of the novelty of the structure, the character-drawing, and 'the truthful delineation of life as it actually is' must have been

based on some knowledge of one or several plays in English translation.

Moreover, Hankin's implicit reference to an ongoing critical debate and to the problematic reception of the Russian's dramas – 'The inexperienced critic and the careless critic – of whom alas there are plenty – say and even think that Tchekoff "cannot write a play"'[8] – seems to indicate the existence of translations well before any Chekhov play was performed on the British stage, or had appeared in print.

In a letter to *The Nation* of 19 December 1908 – an acid reply to William Archer's criticism of his latest play, *The Last of the De Mullins* – Hankin once more promotes the Russian. He reproaches Archer, the leader of the Ibsen faction, for having lost track of the truly progressive drama of 'Tchekof and the moderns'.[9] Archer's biographer Peter Whitebrook, also referring to Hankin's attack, claims that before any Chekhov play had been produced on the English stage,

Hankin and several other dramatists were buzzing with enthusiasm about [Chekhov]. They had heard reports of the Moscow Art Theatre productions and read Constance Garnett's unpublished translation of *The Cherry Orchard*. Archer had not, and Hankin rebuked him for drifting so far from the centre of things that he had become a campaigner without a cause.[10]

With reference to the repertoire of modern European plays at the Court under Barker, Jan McDonald finds surprising the absence of Chekhov's plays. She maintains that his plays were 'certainly known to the Stage Society and there were translations available by Constance Garnett'.[11] However, neither Whitebrook nor McDonald offer any substantial evidence as to the dating of Constance Garnett's *The Cherry Orchard* or the existence of other unpublished translations by her.

Going by the publication dates of her translations of Russian authors, Chekhov's plays (except, of course, Garnett's unpublished translation of *The Cherry Orchard*) were translated fairly late, as they were only published in 1923.

It remains a mystery why there are no records of any interest in Chekhov on the part of Barker before 1914, and we do not know whether he had read or seen any of his dramas before this date. The pioneering Barker scholar Margery Morgan believes that Barker 'does not seem to have known Chekhov's plays before 1914, when he visited Moscow, and so only the later phase of his career as a dramatist [*The Secret Life* (1923) and *His Majesty* (1928)] can have been influenced directly by the Russian writer'.[12] Yet, it appears highly unlikely that a man so involved in the theatrical life of his time, always at the forefront of the theatrical and dramatic avant-garde, could have been unaware of Chekhov the dramatist.

The possible influence of Chekhov on Barker's late Victorian and Edwardian plays is an entirely different matter. Barker had written his first major play, *The Marrying of Ann Leete*, in 1899, well before Chekhov wrote his late plays, *Three Sisters* and *The Cherry Orchard*, which were first performed in 1901 and 1904. Barker worked on *The Voysey Inheritance* between 1903 and 1905, before, it appears, English translations of Chekhov's plays were available – and *Waste* (1906-07) is hardly Chekhovian. The only Edwardian play of Granville Barker's which might have been influenced by Chekhov, presupposing Barker's *unauthenticated* knowledge of the latter's dramatic works, is *The Madras House*, written in 1909.[13]

The records of Barker's critical appreciation of Chekhov date from much later. In *The Exemplary Theatre* Barker refers to him as the master of the 'implicit' method of playwriting, who leaves it to the actor to discover and disclose the subtext, the unwritten and unspoken dialogue[14] – unlike Shaw, in whose plays 'there is apt to be very little written between the lines'.[15] In *On Dramatic Method*, Granville Barker refers to *Three Sisters* and *The Cherry Orchard* as those of Chekhov's dramas in which he had achieved a perfect harmony between form and content. However, the fashion in which the characters 'shape and vitalize the play' Barker considers 'peculiarly Russian'.

Moreover, Barker believes that 'the same manner and the same dramatic method and form will not be so eloquent of English

character or life, or of French or German; it would even falsify it.'[16] This statement would preclude Barker seeing his own work in any proximity to that of Chekhov. Yet an earlier reference, in a letter to William Archer of 1 October 1923, points in a different direction. In this letter, Barker names the later Ibsen as his master – immediately qualifying this statement by adding,

I don't name Tchekov. But (or 'for' or 'though') it was when I saw the Moscow people interpreting Tchekov that I fully realized what I had been struggling towards – and that I saw how much actors *could* add to a play.[17]

His visit to the Moscow Art Theatre and his meeting with Stanislavsky in February 1914 had left a lasting impression on Barker. In his letter to Archer, written nine years later, he clearly expresses his admiration for the work of the great Russian director. Likewise, Barker indicates, though less clearly, his kinship with Chekhov.

The Common Ground

In the early decades of our century only a handful of critics, most notably Desmond MacCarthy and P. P. Howe, pointed out the similarities between Barker's dramatic aesthetic and Chekhov's. MacCarthy likens his dialogue to that of the Russian master, while P. P. Howe also finds a resemblance in their ability to generate atmosphere.[18]

In more recent discussions of Barker's dramatic works, we find various references to Chekhovian techniques, some indicating a general affinity, others noting specific analogies. The director William Gaskill, for example, who was responsible for the production of *The Voysey Inheritance* at the Edinburgh Festival in 1992 and also successfully directed *The Madras House* for the National Theatre in 1977, sees the difference between Barker and Shaw and the resemblance between Barker and Chekhov in the presentation of ideas. Thus, while Shaw's characters function as the mouthpieces of the dramatist, Chekhov's figures convey their own ideas – 'the characters have ideas; but we always see that they're *their* ideas';[19] the same applies to Barker's dramatic figures. Moreover, these ideas are of a tentative nature, and the characters lack confidence as to the appropriateness and effectiveness of their actions – indeed they are even hesitant about taking action at all. In contrast to Shaw, neither Chekhov nor Barker allows his protagonists to offer any unquestioned, definite solution to the problems explored in the dramas.[20]

In his study of Granville Barker, Salenius lists three more points of comparison: 'There is definitely a suggestion of Chekhov in Barker's technique of creating atmosphere through the use of detail, in the fact that the drama in his plays is internal rather than external, and in the careful though seemingly haphazard construction.'[21]

To these some additional considerations could be added. While Barker explores profound problems from his own ironic vantage point, Chekhov, likewise an ironist, dramatizes the human dilemma within the context of a generic blend of the serious and the comic, or, as Richard Peace puts it, 'his comedy mixes laughter with pathos'.[22] Most Barker protagonists are not men of action but of reflection, and are well-intentioned but lacking in drive and determination. In a similar way, Chekhov focuses on his characters' aspirations rather than their achievements. Both playwrights are more interested in the secret lives of their characters than in their outward existence.

In an interview with Julie Morrice, Peter James, who directed *The Madras House* for the Edinburgh Festival in 1992, illustrates the Chekhovian qualities of the play in terms of characterization and the significance of the subtext:

To write a socio-political play populated by people with as much inner life as Chekhovian characters is a difficult and very courageous thing to try for. [Barker] was a staunch Fabian with strong political views which he wanted to express, but at the same time he knew that what went on underneath and behind the words that were being spoken were the things that you ought to be investigating.[23]

The following more detailed comparison will focus on Chekhov's last two plays, *Three Sisters* and *The Cherry Orchard* – without doubt his greatest, and also those first performed in the twentieth century – and on Barker's Edwardian plays, *The Marrying of Ann Leete*, *The Voysey Inheritance*, and *The Madras House*, first performed in 1902, 1905, and 1910 respectively.

Social and Cultural Evolution

In the two latter dramas by Barker, as well as in Chekhov's masterpieces, the takeover or sale of a house, an estate, or a business – i.e., a change in ownership or management – forms the material backbone of the plot and, at the same time, signifies a wider change and evolution: the onset of a new epoch, full of social and cultural repercussions. Seemingly inconclusive endings which actually mark new beginnings are a trademark alike of Chekhov's and Barker's plays: and in both playwrights this structural pattern suggests, in socio-cultural terms, the end of an era and the dawn of a new century.

In *Three Sisters*, Natasha, the provincial social climber, marries the son of the former battery commander. Brutal and ruthless, she gradually assumes control over the house, comes to dominate and deceive her husband, and, ultimately, evicts his sisters. The cultural implications of this usurpation are even more significant than the social ones. Natasha, uneducated but very strong-willed, encounters hardly any resistance from the three sisters, who are educated and highly (perhaps over) refined, but lack energy and resolve.

To an extent, the sisters are aware of this predicament. Masha has come to regard their (over) education as a ballast: 'Knowing three languages in a town like this is an unnecessary luxury. In fact, not even a luxury, but just a sort of useless encumbrance.'[24] Shaken by Natasha's inhumanity, Olga complains, 'any cruel or tactless remark, even the slightest discourtesy, upsets me.' Maurice Valency draws the following conclusion from this opposition of unequal forces:

The cultivated classes, refined to the point where they can no longer endure the struggle for survival, cannot hold their own with the more vigorous social elements which desire to supplant them in the social hierarchy.[25]

In *The Cherry Orchard*, Lopakhin, the son of a former serf, buys the Ranyevsky property. Though lacking Natasha's deviousness, he is just as uneducated, as he himself admits: 'No one taught me anything, my writing is awful, I'm ashamed even to show it to people: it's just like a pig's.' Leaving aside his major speech in Act III, where he briefly displays ruthlessness and self-satisfaction, Lopakhin can essentially be described as a 'peasant turned entrepreneur, awkward, kind, and yet businesslike'.[26]

Gilman – who, not wholly convincingly, attempts to explain away any socio-political-historical dimension in Chekhov's plays – does not explore why Liubov does not take up Lopakhin's proposition for saving the estate. To this problem Valency provides a plausible answer on the basis of the cultural heritage, or (one might say) the cultural burden of the gentry:

By character and background she is precluded from acting like a merchant in this crisis. The psychic impotence and the economic bankruptcy of her class at this period of history are aspects of the same illness. The nobility is at the end of life. It remains only to die nobly, if that is possible.[27]

The Burden of Constraint in Barker's Plays

This idea that the economic and cultural legacy of a class represents an onus is also a significant theme in Barker's plays. Likewise, the transition from the old and familiar to the new and uncertain – a key aspect of the post-Victorian *zeitgeist* – is at the core of Barker's analysis of Edwardian England. From a different perspective, Jan McDonald defines the central thematic concern in the Barker plays as 'the passing of an old order of civilization and the emergence of a new force that is strong and vital'. In particular, 'the plays show the often painful process of transition'.[28] *Three Sisters* and *The Cherry Orchard* would lend themselves to a similar interpretation.

The Marrying of Ann Leete is set at the end of the eighteenth century, also a period of transition. Ann, the daughter of the unscrupulous politician Carnaby Leete – also the declining patriarch of an ancient but impoverished dynasty – refuses to marry Lord John Carp, a suitor chosen by her father for political reasons. Instead, she proposes to and marries the gardener, John Abud. She turns her back on her class, her disintegrating family, and a doomed civilization in order to make a new start: 'We've all been in too great a hurry getting civilized. False dawn. I mean to go back.'[29] As Jan McDonald aptly puts it, 'she "goes back" and, indeed, forward'[30] in forming a union with the strong and healthy gardener.

Apart from the more obvious load of financial troubles Edward has to bear, a major issue in *The Voysey Inheritance* is the oppressive, constraining nature of the cultural Voysey inheritance, representative of that of the upper middle class. It is, not surprisingly, the artist among the Voyseys who voices his discontent most frankly and most pointedly. In Act IV Hugh confides to his brother Edward that his respectable upbringing and the financial support of his father are to blame for his failure as an artist and his lack of individual artistic identity:

Well, what have I really learnt . . . about myself . . . that's the only learning . . . that there's nothing I can do or be but reflects our drawing-room at Chislehurst.

Confronting the entire Voysey clan in Act V, Hugh launches a comprehensive and harsh attack on the middle-class family, its value structure, and its peculiar culture. He envies his elder brother Trenchard, 'who managed to cut [himself] off from his family' and escape 'from tyranny! . . . from hypocrisy! . . . from boredom! . . . from his Happy English Home!' For Hugh all the Voyseys are 'dull, cubbish, uneducated . . . hopelessly middle-class'. This Voysey heritage has had a crippling effect on his development as an artist and a human being: 'I tried to express myself in art . . . and found there was nothing to express. . . . D'you blame me if I wander about in search of a soul of some sort?'

Hugh's wife Beatrice is much more sober and independent than her husband. Though hardly ever sharing his views, she does agree with him on the subject of his family, believing that the Voyseys – and implicitly the upper middle-class family and its culture as a whole – belong to a dying world and have become incapable of regeneration: the family will 'never make any new life for itself.'

This kind of cultural pessimism is counterbalanced by Edward's gradual and painful acceptance of the Voysey inheritance. In a process of change as painful to him as to Chekhov's characters, he has to discard his idealism and adapt his ethical standards to a new situation. The system which he has inherited from his father of investing clients' entrusted money in risky projects and pocketing the surplus interest has rendered the firm virtually bankrupt and puts Edward's principles to the test. Despite its hazards and incalculable results, he eventually faces the task of restoring the accounts. In doing so he ironically takes his father's advice 'to cultivate [his] own sense of right and wrong' – and, as his father predicted, it does make 'a bigger man' of him. Perhaps Edward's maturing does, after all, suggest a certain regenerative potential among the Voyseys.

Philip Madras, the protagonist in *The Madras House*, intends to cast off the burden of the civilization of his class, which obscures a view of the unpleasant realities of life and, essentially, blocks progress and social reform: 'If we can't love the bad as well as the beautiful . . . then we good and clever people are costing the world too much. . . . Rags pay for finery and ugliness for beauty, and sin for virtue.'[31] He also wants to take his daughter Mildred out of 'that precious school' which is 'cultivating Mildred's mind into but another museum'. Philip wishes to have her brought up in a manner that also opens her eyes to the unsavoury side of life, 'even if it means not adding her to the aristocracy of good feeling and good taste . . . the very latest of class distinctions'.

Likewise, Philip attempts to convince his wife Jessica, 'an epitome of all that aesthetic culture can do for a woman', of the necessity of freeing herself from over-refinement, a process inextricably linked with her liberation and emancipation as a woman: 'There's a price to be paid for free womanhood, I think . . . and how many of you ladies are willing to pay it? Come out and be common women among us common men?'

Labour and Parasitism

The themes of work and of parasitism in the wider context of the social order are explored in Chekhov as in Barker. In their repeated speeches in *Three Sisters* on the importance of hard work, Irina, Tusenbach, and Vershinin postulate its vitalizing and ennobling effects. The offspring of a class 'who despised work' – of a parasitic class, bored and unhappy – they see work as a panacea for all their problems and as a guarantor of happiness in the future. However, as Gilman observes,

the work they invoke so ardently is still to come and, like the future itself, its reality exists only in their conversation; its solicitation is that of an idea, a piece of ideality. And again like the future their talk about work serves to relieve and deflect present discontents, to project them onto an agency or principle of healing.[32]

In a similar way, the three sisters' nostalgically transfigured Moscow is a vision to compensate for present malaise and to sustain hope for the future.

In *The Cherry Orchard*, the representatives of the Russian gentry live on the work of their peasants and the money of their creditors. Here it is Trofimov, the eternal student, who defines the parasitic existence of Anya's family:

Just think, Anya: your grandfather, your great grandfather and all your forefathers were serf owners – they owned living souls. Don't you see human beings gazing at you from every cherry tree in your orchard, from every leaf and every tree-trunk, don't you hear voices?. . . . They owned living souls – and it has perverted you all, those who came before you, and you who are living now, so that your mother, your uncle and even you yourself no longer realize that you're living in debt, at other people's expense, at the expense of people you don't admit further than the kitchen.

Trofimov believes that one has to atone for one's past by 'suffering, by extraordinary, unceasing exertion'. Yet his inflated rhetoric indicates that Chekhov does not share this pseudo-revolutionary posture. On the other hand, although he gives him a comic touch, he does not make the eternal student a butt of ridicule. In any case, Trofimov's sermons closely resemble the oratory of Tusenbach and Vershinin, thus exposing themselves as abstract doctrines of salvation.

Superficially different yet fundamentally similar concepts of parasitism are examined in Barker's plays. Almost all the characters in *The Voysey Inheritance* thus live 'on the proceeds of unearned income'.[33] The cosy lifestyle of the Voysey family and the education of the younger Voyseys has been paid for from the illegal profits old Voysey made by embezzling his clients' money. Mr. Booth, who takes great pride in his gentlemanly existence – defined as never having done a stroke of work in his entire life – has lived well on the interest his considerable, mostly inherited fortune yields.

Even Peacey, the head clerk in the office of Voysey and Son, has increased his income by receiving hush-money from old Voysey. It is Alice Maitland, living comfortably on unearned income herself, who quotes her guardian's ironical yet pragmatic definition of the ethical grounds for the distribution of money in a capitalist society:

You've no particular right to your money. You've not earned it or deserved it in any way. And don't be either surprised or annoyed when any enterprising person tries to get it from you. He has at least as much right to it as you have . . . if he can use it better perhaps he has more right.

We would err, however, in reading the play as a Fabian critique of capitalism. For while Barker may analyze the peculiarities of the economic system from an ironic perspective, as in its similarity to gambling, he does not reject it as such.

Exploitation and Dependence

The Madras House is concerned with a different brand of parasitism, exploitation and dependence. The first act, which, in Chekhovian terms, could be entitled *Six Sisters*, centres on the six unmarried Huxtable daughters, who are sacrificed on the altar of Victorian–Edwardian propriety and class-consciousness. The drapery shop of Roberts and Huxtable, where the second act is set, can – just like the Huxtable drawing-room – be compared to a prison: 'The prisoners, both men and women, are the employees who not only work in the shop but are victims of the "living-in" system: they live on the premises, sleeping in supervised dormitories.'[34]

The mannequins at the fashion show in the third act are exploited as objects, and in a wider context the entire fashion industry thrives on the exploitation of women. The prospective buyer of the Madras House, the American Eustace Perrin State, sees the fashion business as contributing to the emancipation of woman, in that financially more independent women can express themselves through dress. On the other hand, the entrepreneur does not lose sight of economic perspectives: after all, 'the Middle Class Women of England . . . form one of the greatest Money Spending Machines the world has ever seen'.

One can certainly join Jan McDonald in recognizing the inherent cynicism of this position: 'The States of the world will continue, under the guise of liberating women, to exploit them for financial gain.'[35] Unlike State, Philip Madras is a *genuine* champion of the emancipation of women. He decides to sell his share in the firm and turns down the offer of a directorship, since he has 'grown to see the family business as a parasite attacking what is weakest in women while encouraging them into further exploitation'.[36]

Philip Madras does not lead an idle life as do the characters in *Three Sisters* who preach the gospel of work, yet he intends to devote himself to a more meaningful occupation. Philip aspires 'to save [his] soul alive' by doing 'dull, hard work' on the County Council. But the notion of the dignifying, redeeming effects of work is undercut in Chekhov and in Barker in similar ways. In the minds of Chekhov's characters work is a matter for the future, just as are Philip's efforts at social reform. And, although Philip Madras appears to be determined to get on the County Council, he does not do so during the play. As Peter James observes: 'The play begins with him talking about doing things and ends with him talking about doing things, and that's all you can say really, you don't see him do them.'[37]

In the revised version of the play of 1925, Barker moreover seems to have blunted the edge of Philip's reforming zeal. Before defining the sort of work he intends to do as a member of the Council, Philip now characterizes himself 'as a visionary [who is] all for compromise. I'm going into politics . . . the great art of compromise.' Like Chekhov, he ironizes the champion of work and reform.

Only in *The Voysey Inheritance* do we actually see Edward doing hard and unpleasant work. Yet while the unscrupulous father took great pleasure and great pride in his own cunning juggling of the system, the scrupulous son is only motivated by his sense of duty and responsibility to embark on 'that dreary round'. Yet, in contrast to Chekhov, Barker's protagonist *is* transformed by the Herculean task of imposing order on the anarchic financial structures of the firm. Furthermore, the matured Edward has gained the respect, the support, and, it appears, the hand of Alice Maitland. Dennis Kennedy's reading of their joint project has a somewhat inappropriately heroic ring: 'Together they will attack old Voysey's mess, finding personal salvation in holy dedication to a secret cause.'[38]

The endings of Chekhov's and of Barker's plays do not mark a destination but a departure. However, while Chekhov's plays end on a note of uncertainty tempered by a glimpse of hope, Barker's end on a note of optimism tempered by a touch of irony. Maurice Valency here characterizes the lack of finality in Chekhovian drama in almost poetic terms:

Man ends; but his story is endless. Chekhov's plays are not finished. When the curtain has fallen, the play goes on; there is still the sense of flux. We say farewell, and the brigade moves on toward other horizons.[39]

In the last act of *Three Sisters*, the prospects are far from bright for most of the characters. The brigade actually moves on – including Vershinin, who will cling to his belief in a paradise to come. Tusenbach has been killed in the duel; now he cannot (or rather, he need not) act on his conviction of gaining happiness through hard work. The three sisters are 'left alone . . . to start [their] lives all over again'. Masha will have to overcome her grief at Vershinin's departure and resign herself to the same old life with her forbearing husband. Olga will go on overworking herself as a headmistress. Irina will leave and find a position as a schoolteacher; she will 'give [her] life to people who need it'.

Endings as Beginnings

At the end of the play, Chebutykin's nonsensical song and cynical comment, 'Nothing matters!' is juxtaposed with Olga's desire to find out the purpose of human suffering, of human existence. Perhaps the play suggests that this very quest for knowledge which sustains mankind in its never-ending, reiterated voyage of discovery, *is* the purpose of human life.

The departure act of *The Cherry Orchard* may be seen in a similar context, albeit with a different emphasis. It is not only an act of leave-taking, but also an act of coming to terms with the realities of change. The representatives of the old order are bidding farewell to their familiar world, which is now being reshaped by the exponents of the new order. 'Liubov will have a few more spasms of longing and nostalgia'[40] before turning her back on the past. Varya has found a position as a housekeeper. Gayev brightly announces that he is now an employee of a bank – though his habitual indolence and his grandiloquent reference to himself as a financier may raise doubts as to his future there.

The happiest of the family is young Anya: for her the leave-taking really does mark the beginning of a new life. Only the old servant Firs is accidentally left behind. In his own way, Firs is the embodiment of the old order, who regards the emancipation of the serfs as a great misery which, decades before, brought confusion into the social order. Richard Gilman provides a convincing reading of the final stage image, of Firs locked up in the now deserted house – to be precise, in the former nursery:

Everybody's gone, off to some new scene or phase, moving, however uncertainly, toward the *next thing*. But there's no next thing for aged Firs. He sums up an era, finishes it off. He'll die with the house, a victim technically of Yasha's thoughtlessness but really of time in its casual dispositionings. Throughout the play he's been composed almost entirely of memories; now they're used up. His being abandoned makes us think, all at the same time, of mortality, chance, the end of things, the beginning, change.[41]

It is also a feature of Barker's plays that they end with a new beginning, however vaguely it may be sketched. Ann Leete has left the aristocratic world to start a new life with the gardener Abud. This experiment, this real challenge for the protagonist, concludes *The Marrying of Ann Leete*. The final scene does not anticipate a romantically blissful union; for Ann it will mean hard work, bearing children, and subservience to her husband. None the less, Ann Leete has entered this new world by and from choice.

At the end of *The Voysey Inheritance* the now matured Edward Voysey is finally ready to shoulder the inherited burden of fraudulent financial transactions, with the support of Alice Maitland. However, the options, ranging from bankruptcy and imprisonment to an eventual solution of the complex problems, are only intimated, as is his marriage to Alice. While Edward still does not work on a strictly legal basis, the objective has changed radically, from illegal profit-making to illegal reparation – certainly a kind of departure, though the destination remains unknown.

An Integral Equivocation

In a way, the first act of *The Madras House*, with its comically repeated entrances and exits, arrivals and departures, could be read as a parody of Chekhovian dramaturgy. This act, overcrowded with characters, introduces us to the Huxtable seraglio, presided over by the matronly Mrs. Huxtable – in the Edinburgh Festival production of 1992, appropriately and suggestively dressed like Queen Victoria.

The six Huxtable daughters, defenceless against the strictures imposed by outworn upper middle-class codes of conduct, are doomed to perpetual spinsterhood. Their existence is exclusively shaped by others. In striking and significant contrast, the final scene of Act IV, the long duologue between Jessica and Philip, delineates a future of social reform and independent womanhood.

Jessica has not only grasped the freedom to transform her life, but she is supported, even urged, by her husband to embrace the cause of the genuine liberation and emancipation of women. While the ambitions of the intellectual reformer Philip Madras are spelt out clearly at the end of the play, their translation into action remains a matter of speculation. The dialogue breaks off in mid-sentence, 'for really there is no end to the subject'. And the revised version of *The Madras House* ends on an even more tentative and enigmatic note:

JESSICA. Poor Phil! (*She pats his cheek, then kisses it. 'Poor Phil' is but pretty irony, of course; such a charming home as he has, such a charming wife! As long as he'll only see his visions in the domestic fire . . . !*)

Analogous thematic concerns and structural patterns attest the affinity between Barker and Chekhov. Both explore social and cultural phenomena in an epoch of transition. A new beginning in a new century is reflected in a new dramaturgy. The equivocal endings mirror the caution with which the characters look into the future, and suggest an expedition into unknown territory.

At the turn of the nineteenth and twentieth centuries kindred spirits in Russia and in England simultaneously and independently conceived a dramatic aesthetic which placed them at the forefront of modernism in drama. In response to the question mark in the title of this paper, it would appear appropriate to give the curtain line to

William Gaskill: 'Granville Barker is the first great English Chekhovian.'[42]

Notes and References

1. Sam Walters in an interview with Dennis Kennedy, 'Being a Director is Like Being a Detective', in Jan McDonald and Leslie Hill, eds., *Harley Granville Barker: an Edinburgh Retrospective, 1992* (Glasgow: Theatre Studies Publications, 1993), p. 98.

2. Of his early major plays, Barker wrote *The Marrying of Ann Leete* in 1899 and *The Voysey Inheritance* from 1903 to 1905. See 'A List of Writings', compiled by Frederick May and Margery M. Morgan, in C. B. Purdom, *Harley Granville Barker: Man of the Theatre, Dramatist, and Scholar* (London: Rockliff, 1955), p. 294.

3. The first English translations published in Britain were by Marian Fell (1912), George Calderon (1912), Julius West (1915, 1916), and Constance Garnett (1923, 1926, 1929). An early translation of a Chekhov play to come out in the United States was by Max S. Mandell (of *The Cherry Garden*, 1908). In some sources Isabel F. Hapgood is credited with a translation of *The Seagull* (1905); however, it appears that this is only a synopsis of 15 pages.

4. *The Seagull*, Glasgow Repertory Theatre, November 1909; *The Bear*, Kingsway, May 1911; *The Cherry Orchard*, Stage Society at the Aldwych, May 1911; *The Seagull*, Adelphi Play Society at the Little Theatre, March 1912; *Uncle Vanya*, Stage Society at the Aldwych, May 1914. See Jan McDonald, 'Productions of Chekhov's Plays in Britain before 1914', *Theatre Notebook*, XXXIV, No. 1 (1980), p. 25. This article was reprinted in Patrick Miles, ed., *Chekhov on the British Stage* (Cambridge University Press, 1993) under the title, 'Chekhov, Naturalism, and the Drama of Dissent: Productions of Chekhov's Plays in Britain before 1914', p. 29-42.

5. Dan H. Laurence, ed., *Bernard Shaw: Collected Letters 1898-1910* (London: Reinhardt, 1972), p. 569.

6. Letter to George Moore, undated [assigned to October 1911], in Dan H. Laurence, ed., *Bernard Shaw: Collected Letters 1911-1925* (London: Reinhardt, 1985), p. 53.

7. Hankin, 'The Stage Society: the "Moscow School" of Drama', *Academy*, LXXII (15 June 1907), p. 585.

8. Hankin, *Academy*, p. 585.

9. Hankin, quoted in Peter Whitebrook, *William Archer: a Biography* (London: Methuen, 1993), p. 280.

10. Peter Whitebrook, *William Archer*, p. 280. Constance Garnett's translation was used for the Stage Society production in 1911.

11. Jan McDonald, *The 'New Drama' 1900–1914* (London: Macmillan, 1986), p. 15.

12. Margery M. Morgan, *A Drama of Political Man: a Study in the Plays of Harley Granville Barker* (London: Sidgwick and Jackson, 1961), p. 21.

13. For the dates of composition, see May and Morgan, 'A List of Writings', p. 294.

14. See Harley Granville Barker, *The Exemplary Theatre* (London: Chatto and Windus, 1922), p. 140.

15. Barker, *The Exemplary Theatre*, p. 134.

16. Harley Granville Barker, *On Dramatic Method* (New York: Hill and Wang, 1956), p. 186-7, reprint of edition published by Sidgwick and Jackson, 1931.

17. Letter to William Archer of 1 October 1923, in Eric Salmon, ed., *Granville Barker and His Correspondents: a Selection of Letters by Him and to Him* (Detroit: Wayne State University Press, 1986), p. 102.

18. See McDonald, *Theatre Notebook*, p. 28.

19. Gaskill, quoted in Cary M. Mazer, 'The Voysey Inheritance', in *Harley Granville Barker: an Edinburgh Retrospective, 1992*, p. 61.

20. Cf. Mazer, 'The Voysey Inheritance', p. 61.

21. Elmer W. Salenius, *Harley Granville Barker* (Boston: Twayne, 1982), p. 109-10.

22. Richard Peace, in Thomas Eekman, ed., *Critical Essays on Anton Chekhov* (Boston: Hall, 1989), p. 127.

23. Julie Morrice, 'Character Witnesses', in *Scotland on Sunday Edinburgh International Festival Study Guide: Harley Granville Barker*, 26 April 1992, p. 13.

24. Anton Chekhov, *Plays*, trans. Elisaveta Fen (Harmondsworth: Penguin, 1959), p. 263. Subsequent quotations are from this edition.

25. Maurice Valency, *The Breaking String: the Plays of Anton Chekhov* (New York: Schocken, reprint 1983), p. 220. Beverly Hahn argues that it is not so much the likes of Natasha who pose a threat to civilization: 'As civilized people surrounded by, and in some ways embodying, an almost defunct culture, the sisters make us aware of the dilemma . . . of cultured refinement working unconsciously towards its own defeat.' See Beverly Hahn, 'Three Sisters', in René and Nonna D. Wellek, eds., *Chekhov: New Perspectives* (Englewood Cliffs: Prentice-Hall, 1984), p. 145.

26. Richard Gilman, *Chekhov's Plays: an Opening into Eternity* (New Haven: Yale University Press, 1995), p. 222.

27. Valency, *The Breaking String*, p. 270.

28. McDonald, *The 'New Drama'*, p. 56.

29. Dennis Kennedy, ed., *Plays by Harley Granville Barker* (Cambridge University Press, 1987), p. 82. Subsequent quotations from *The Marrying of Ann Leete* and *The Voysey Inheritance* are from this edition.

30. McDonald, *The 'New Drama'*, p. 62.

31. Harley Granville Barker, *The Madras House*, ed. Margery M. Morgan (London: Eyre Methuen, 1977), p. 131. Subsequent quotations from the play are from this edition.

32. Gilman, *Chekhov's Plays*, p. 179.

33. McDonald, *The 'New Drama'*, p. 72.

34. Eric Salmon, *Granville Barker: a Secret Life* (London: Heinemann, 1983), p. 162.

35. McDonald, *The 'New Drama'*, p. 99.

36. Kennedy, *Granville Barker and the Dream of Theatre* (Cambridge University Press, 1985), p. 113.

37. 'Cans of Worms', *Plays International*, VIII, No. 2 (September 1992), p. 13.

38. Dennis Kennedy, 'Introduction' to his edition of *Plays by Harley Granville Barker* (Cambridge University Press, 1987), p. 13.

39. Valency, *The Breaking String*, p. 297.

40. Gilman, *Chekhov's Plays*, p. 238.

41. Ibid., p. 241.

42. Gaskill quoted in Morrice, 'Character Witnesses', p. 13.

Frank Bren

Connections and Crossovers: Cinema and Theatre in Hong Kong

From the run-up to its return to Chinese rule in July 1997 to the stock-market crash in October, Hong Kong has seldom been out of the news during the past year. But the attention paid to its political and economic provenance has not been matched by much interest in its cultural output – despite the existence in Hong Kong of a cinema industry with a prodigious output now approaching ten thousand films. Although a professional theatre has been a relatively more recent development, the connections between film and theatre in Hong Kong have always been close – from the film adaptations of Cantonese opera in the 1930s, through the 'female' films of the post-war period and the western following for Bruce Lee's *kung fu* movies, to the present dominance of the cross-generic production company, Springtime, in the 1990s, with a creative interest in its own past which verges on the metatheatrical. Frank Bren, who is presently living and working in Hong Kong, here captures something of the history and the distinctive flavour of the overlapping movie and theatre industries, and assesses why the relationship remains mutually profitable in artistic as well as economic terms.

ON THE EVENING of 8 January 1992, two thugs wielding knives and guns charged into a Hong Kong film laboratory and demanded negatives from the stunned employees. The thieves obviously knew what they wanted, and zeroed in on the cans marked *All's Well, Ends Well*, a new comedy directed by Clifton Ko Chi-sum.

The scattered reels were mostly for blockbuster films soon opening for the Lunar New Year, a cash-happy season for Hong Kong cinemas. *All's Well* was widely tipped to be top of the heap, since it starred some of the territory's top draws in the comic actor Stephen Chow Sing-chi, the ever-popular Maggie Cheung Man-yuk, and the pop heart-throb Leslie Cheung Gwok-wing.[1]

The thieves grabbed just two reels – a mere fragment of the entire negative – and ignored the rest as they quit the premises like saboteurs who had swiped left-only footwear from a shoe shop. The entire film industry was up in arms over this latest outrage – the last straw in a series of rip-offs, extortions, and violence inflicted by the triads on Hong Kong's show people. But such partial sabotage was new, since the usual method is either to extort 'location'

fees during shoots or to pressure 'name' stars into headlining quickies – financed by the triads – at heavily cut rates.

Fed up, a crowd of the biggest names in the business, including Jackie Chan, Maggie Cheung, and director Philip Chan (a former policeman), took to the Hong Kong streets on 15 January in a show against violence, marching from the Furama Hotel to Police Headquarters, two districts away in Arsenal Skeet, Wanchai. According to the *Hong Kong Standard*, Leslie Cheung was under police protection. Ironically, some of the angry young men had made fortunes in roles which semi-glorified the triads on screen.

In April and May, two murders of local producers raised film industry fears to a peak, although these professional 'hits' were apparently unrelated to the march. Some have said that the subsequent decline in the business finally drove the triads away. Meanwhile, a re-cut *All's Well, Ends Well* eventually grossed HK$48 million in the territory alone – a near record at the time – confirming the Midas touch of its director, Clifton Ko.

In spite of that success, Ko became increasingly concerned about the signs of a

Two stars of the post-war 'golden age' of Hong Kong cinema. Top: Li Li-hua, whose career began in Peking opera in the late 1930s. Bottom: Tsi Lo-lin, whose early training was in Cantonese opera.

'decline' in Hong Kong cinema – and not just because of the triads. The stars themselves were over-priced, other costs were in a steep incline, and many bad movies, sold on star names alone, were beginning to drive audiences away. 'Now everyone talks about Hong Kong cinema's decline', claimed an associate. 'But Clifton said it five years ago and wanted to break new ground.' The 'golden age' was at an end.

This was roughly the point at which a new relationship between Hong Kong's professional theatre and cinema began, co-inciding with a boom in Cantonese drama and the attraction of first-time audiences to the theatre. Space permits only a synoptic overview of Hong Kong's surprisingly complex film industry, past and present, outside this relationship .

The industry's 'golden age' and 'decline' are both relative. Many abroad would kill for the position of the Hong Kong cinema, which, in 1996, still out-earned all foreign films combined at any local box office, Hollywood's included. In fact, there have been three or four 'golden ages' before and after the Second World War. This one was roughly coincident in time with John Woo's cycle of gangster films, starting with *A Better Tomorrow* (1986) and ending with *Hardboiled* (1992). Woo, of course, has since launched a successful career in Hollywood.[2]

Until the Japanese occupation, from 1941 to 1945, Hong Kong had produced just over 600 theatrical films, only ten of which survive today. By 1938, the colony was already one of the world's most prolific film centres, a position it quickly regained just after the war and has sustained until the present.

Many films exist from the second 'golden' period, from the late 1940s to the mid-1960s – an era dominated by unforgettable female stars, many of them (Bai Guang, Zhou Xuan, Li Li-hua) part of the influx from Shanghai which was especially intense during the late 1940s. In a reversal of the present situation, the writer Tsai Kuo-jing (of the 1950s) notes that Li Li-hua would be paid up to HK$75,000 per film – which might be half the budget – whereas leading men could expect perhaps HK$10,000.[3]

The four female singers, identified by the colours of their costumes (from left to right, red, yellow, white, and blue), whose friendship over four decades is nostalgically dramatized in Raymond To's *I Have a Date with Spring*.

Prolonged exposure to these 'female' films of the 1950s and 1960s[4] has created a nostalgia for people like Tsi Lo-lin, Pak Yin, Grace Chang, Yeh Feng, Siao Fong Fong (still active), Lin Dai, and Betty Loh Tih similar to that for, say, Barbara Stanwyck and Jean Arthur. This is the star system (a very glamorous one) at work. But these stars were also excellent screen actors, many groomed as such through classes run by the studios or simply honed through so many film appearances – up to or over twenty per annum. This era was succeeded by the 'new' martial arts period of swordplay and *kung fu*.

Theatre Gives Blood

Apart from the 1950s and early 1960s there seems to have been little vital connection between live theatre and the cinema – until 1993, in which year Clifton Ko acquired the film rights to an unusual stage musical, *I Have a Date with Spring*, written by Hong Kong's leading playwright, Raymond To Kwok-wai.[5] To's play used a 'present-day' nightclub as a time tunnel through which he

flashed back to the 1960s, from there moving forward to dramatize the friendships of four female singers, individually identified by the colours white, red, blue, and yellow. The play builds to a moving finale when the survivors (white and yellow) revisit the club, whose new decor contains four neon butterflies – white, red, blue, and yellow – as a kind of climactic spiritual reunion.[6] To's text was suited to shifting musical tastes – rock, jazz, pop – either 'hard' or dripping with sentiment. These were not only time signatures but 'entertainments' in themselves, an approach typical of this prolific writer.

Actor-director Ko Tin-lung had originally staged *Spring* for the Hong Kong Repertory Theatre – then (1993) as now the major full-time company in the territory. It was an enormous hit and in came the film offers. However, Ko's promise to use the original cast – lacking any stars – in his film discouraged potential backers, in spite of his enviable track record.

The director went ahead anyway with support from the Media Asia Group – a new Warner Communications-style company with

cess', is unprecedented in Hong Kong. Whereas, according to Ko, most Hong Kong films have a budget of around HK$1 million for promotion, for its second theatre production – To's *That's Entertainment* (1996) – Springtime bought HK$5 million worth of advertising – the company itself spending HK$3 million, with the rest coming through sponsorship, including a HK$1 million deal with the Hang Seng Bank.

But the key to the company's success is the criss-crossing of plays between spectacular productions in the Lyric Theatre and the low-budget films either produced or directed by Ko. In the case of To's play, *Mad Phoenix*, the film and live versions were running concurrently last year. In April 1997, during a rehearsal at their premises in Kowloon, Ko cheerily introduced the *Mad Phoenix* cast, chuckling, as he could afford to: 'Now I have two strong legs – one in cinema, the other in theatre!'

'You Saw the Movie, Now See the Play'

Ko's partners in Springtime (more properly, 'Springtime Production Film Company Ltd') are the theatre director Ko Tin-lung and the writer Raymond To. Following their success with the film *Have a Date With Spring*, they promptly re-staged the play in 1995, attracting 70,000 patrons for an unprecedented 70 shows. 'They came because of the movie', Ko Tin-lung insists. 'Before that film, few people came to the theatre in Hong Kong because they had a wrong notion of it as boring, with exaggerated acting. But they liked the film, and if we hadn't re-staged it live we'd have missed a great chance to cultivate this new audience. We created the demand.'

Springtime has wrought a Cantonese mini-Broadway on the Hong Kong scene, merging cinema and theatre in marketing, scripting, and attracting new audiences, not to mention generating new work for actors – with, as Clifton Ko acknowledges, the waves of trained talent now emerging from the Academy for Performing Arts (APA) providing a strong backbone for the large-cast shows currently favoured by his company.

separate production, distribution, and financing arms – and most of his own money. When the film opened in April 1994, the wise predicted a swift death, but with careful nurturing in one or two cinemas and the help of word of mouth, it ran for twenty weeks, grossing four or five times its cost, with two of its 'unknowns', Alice Lau and Lo Koonlan, winning best performance statuettes at the Hong Kong Film Awards for their parts in the film.[7]

From these circumstances arose 'Springtime Productions', one of the most remarkable commercial stage companies in Hong Kong – or anywhere – in terms of its special links to the cinema. Springtime is squarely committed to the star system – but also to 'entertainment' as a sweetener for basically serious works. Most of these, so far, have been by Raymond To.

Springtime is by no means the first commercial drama company in Hong Kong, nor the first to use film or pop stars to lure bums onto seats. But the scale of the operation, and Springtime's ability to 'spend for suc-

Opposite page: Josephine Siao Fong Fong, who emerged as a teen star of the 'female' movies of the 1960s. Above: detail from the poster for *Sumo Do, Sumo Don't*, adapted from the movie as a stage production by Springtime Productions in 1996.

That's Entertainment, with sixty shows in 1996, typified the company's approach by using pop star/film actor Jordan Chan, who was by then cresting on his appearances in films like *Young and Dangerous* (which romanticized the triads). He and other 'names' drew in some 60,000 playgoers, half of them first-timers – as revealed by the show of hands from the audience taken by the partners after each performance.

Mad Phoenix was a textbook example of a mutual transfusion between the theatre and cinema. Clifton Ko timed the release of his film to promote the play at the Lyric in May–June 1997. It was a logical ploy: you've seen the movie, now see the play – and, partly, *vice versa*. An intriguing story about the almost forgotten Cantonese playwright and filmmaker Nam Hoi Sap Sam Long, *Mad Phoenix* also strengthens the vigorous ties between film and theatre from the very beginnings of Cantonese cinema – the first Hong Kong feature film, *Zuangxi Tests His Wife* (1913), having been adapted from a Cantonese Opera.[8]

Ko and his partners are aiming at an annual attendance of 150,000 – about twice that of the Hong Kong Repertory Theatre

(HKRT) – and it seems they will reach their target. They turned up the heat last year with *four* productions. In July, the company introduced Japanese wrestling on stage in *Sumo Do Sumo Don't*, adapted from the hit Japanese film by Masayuki Suo, along with inserts paying homage to his other films like *Shall We Dance?*[9]

The piece was refreshingly free from the usual cheap shots at the sport, and Masayuki himself was invited to see the show. Directed by Lee Chun Leung and penned by Leung Ka Kit, *Sumo Do Sumo Don't* toured as a 'family musical' around Hong Kong's civic centres. It was the first Springtime play *not* written by To. By July, the most impressive show billboard in town was for *Pygmalion* – by Shaw, not To – drawing attention to the company's November treat.

Spaces and Faces

The partners complain of just one major handicap – the lack of permanent theatres for individual companies in Hong Kong. Daniel S. P. Yang, the Artistic Director of the HKRT, agrees. The Hong Kong 'Rep' operates out of Urban Council premises in

Sheung Wan on Hong Kong island. Although it is the territory's major company, offering long-term contracts to actors, it has no permanent theatre, but, like Springtime, has to book available 'slots' in either central venues like the Studio or Grand theatres of the Hong Kong Cultural Centre, Kowloon, or the 'regional' spaces further out. In that sense, it it still living out of a suitcase two decades after its foundation. Hong Kong's two other main subsidized companies, Chung Ying and Exploration Theatre, share the problem of homelessness.

The APA'S Lyric Theatre, says Clifton Ko, is the only venue that presently meets Springtime's needs. But it is a shared venue with is available to local companies for only around thirty days each year. In May–June 1997, the sellout of the company's *Mad Phoenix* obviously called for an extension of the season, but there was no available slot until almost a year later. Smash-hit shows could not be extended in the normal way.[10]

In August–September, the company presented To's *Magic is the Moonlight*, a 'flashback' drama that starts off in a 'present-day' (1987) karaoke bar on the site of a famous pre-war nightclub in Shanghai. Structured like *Spring*, and directed by the actor Tang Shu-wing, *Magic* was the company's fifth production, peeling back fifty years to pre-Liberation Shanghai, under siege from Japan, then moving forward in time through a love triangle featuring the film and stage stars, Cecilia Yip, Lo Koon-lan, and Tse Kwan-ho.

Cecilia Yip's film career has included the hilarious 'mystery woman' in the film, *Peace Hotel* (1995) – playing opposite Chow Yun-fat, just before that actor left for Hollywood – and an earlier role in *Centre Stage*. She had previously twice been named 'best actress' at the annual Hong Kong Film Awards. Lo, though a stage actress, is a three-time nominee and one-time winner (as 'best supporting actress') at the same awards, while Tse, who played the title role in both the film and the stage versions of *Mad Phoenix*, is the company's first contract performer. Such an ensemble admirably fits the Springtime bill: serious talent for demanding roles, but with 'names' to pull in sceptical punters.

Prior to directing *Magic is the Moonlight*, Tang Shu-wing staged two re-runs of his own works, one co-devised and both created out of 'small' newspaper stories with equal dramatic and absurdist potential. Directing *Magic*, he says, was his first 'straight' commercial job – having spent six years in Paris, before returning to Hong Kong in 1992. He talks passionately about theatre aesthetics, which he studied at the Sorbonne, not just in a production's external presentation but in the less visible dynamic – the dramatic mindset – that makes a particular play work between actor and onlooker. The two 'newspaper' stories are good examples.

His co-devised *Two Men in a No Man's Land* used real-life 'news' – well known in Hong Kong – about two Hong Kongers, falsely arrested on drugs charges, who spent two years in a Manila gaol awaiting their appearance in court. When they were finally exonerated, the courthouse was burned down, destroying their legal papers. Back they went for another two years, awaiting another appearance. Even then their families had to pay for their 'state accommodation' before they could finally be released. 'It was so absurd, so tragic', said Tang. He and another actor devised a comi-tragedy in a semi-cabaret style around the affair, with the audiences voting on the jail terms – and, as a result, the length and style of each night's performance.

Tang then spent time on the mainland with the Guangdong Theatre Puppet Company, learning its manipulation techniques (which should, he admits, take years). Tang used the experience in his dramatization of a mainland murder case involving three women – two murderers and a victim. The result, *Three Women in Pearl River Delta*, employed three actresses and three puppets – the former representing their minds, the latter their bodies – in a kind of philosophical, ghosts-in-hell murder enquiry which became a big hit critically and with audiences. Such brave ventures are generally subsidized either by the Urban Council or by the Arts Development Council, the equivalent in Hong Kong of the Arts Council in Britain.

Promotional leaflet for *Magic is the Moonlight*, with (left to right) Cecilia Yip, Tse Kwan-ho, and Lo Koon-lan.

The original play versions of *Spring* and *Mad Phoenix* were both directed by Ko Tin-lung for the Hong Kong Repertory Theatre. The 'Rep' was established in 1978 as the territory's first full-time professional company with full-time contracts for actors and a year-round repertoire of plays. Initially these were mainly translations of foreign plays – classic and contemporary – but the mix is now about equal between Chinese-language and translated foreign works.

Young Playwrights for a Young Theatre

The artistic director, Dr. Daniel S. P. Yang, emphasized that the twentieth anniversary season of 1997-98 consisted of 'all Chinese plays', four out of the six being Hong Kong originals and three of these specially commissioned works by local playrights: 'This is a fantastic percentage.' A native of Wuxi, Jiangxu, in China, Dr. Yang has twice been the company's artistic director, though he was trained in a different theatrical tradition, having been a Peking Opera and Kunju Opera actor in China, where he specialized in the 'Xiaosheng' or young man role.

I saw what is perhaps the most spectacular item of this anniversay season – a revival of *Tales of the Walled City*, a sumptuous co-operation between the HKRT, the Hong Kong Chinese Orchestra, and the Hong Kong Dance Company. This is a hundred-year view of the Walled City – part of Kowloon, but a strange no-man's-land governed neither by Britain nor China, which was demolished in the early 1990s.

Chung Ying (literally, 'Chinese-English') was set up in 1979 under the auspices of the British Council as a theatre-in-education company. It staged its first Cantonese play in 1981, and is one of the SAR'S brightest ensembles – but, although TIE is now just one of its functions, it has, like other companies, yet to be housed in a permanent theatre.[11] Its first Artistic Director, Glen Walford, was succeeeded by Colin George in 1982, by Bernard Goss in 1984, and by Chris Johnson in 1988. – Ko becoming its first Chinese artistic director in 1993.

For the company's fifteenth anniversary season (1994-95), Ko commissioned all new works in Cantonese – all *Chung* and no *Ying*, in which sense the 'handover' of 1997 had already happened in the performing arts – the cinema included. (Chung Ying was a British caterpillar that became a Cantonese butterfly.)

Exploration Theatre, established in 1982, is the third of Hong Kong's subsidized professional companies, and the only one of the three to have matured from an amateur into a professional company – after 1989, when it achieved its first major subsidy. Karley Ng, the founder, remains its artistic director, also working under the playwriting *nom de plume* of Mok Hei. Ng's and the company's primary goal is 'to nurture the development of original works and playwrights in the soil of Hong Kong theatre'. In August, the company staged its fifteenth anniversary work, *One Night King*, written by the ubiquitous Raymond To – in this way underscoring the close links between the three subsidized companies and Springtime Productions.

'We see things this way', says Ko Tin-lung. 'China has less than a century of what we call modern theatre as influenced by Henrik Ibsen. Hong Kong is even younger – we began professionally in the 1970s.' Ko himself began as an amateur in 1972 at a time when (disregarding Cantonese opera) there was no full-time professional theatre in Hong Kong. Having joined the Hong Kong Repertory Theatre as a professional actor in 1983, he became its assistant artistic director before his appointment at Chung Ying.

Is Raymond To the Neil Simon of Hong Kong? He has had at least five of his plays made into films – including *Hu Dou Men* (*Stage Door*, 1995), which starred the remarkable Josephine Siao Fong Fong as a Cantonese opera star giving one last performance before retiring with her family to Australia. The tone of To's plays is more like that of the emotion-packed Cantonese weepies and comedies of the 1950s – that truly 'golden age' in the history of Hong Kong cinema.

Contrary to first appearances, there are in fact several other young playwrights at work or in development in Hong Kong. 'But it took us more than ten years to produce one Raymond To', says Ko Tin-lung. 'Raymond is the top playwright in Hong Kong but, like many of us, was never trained in theatre. He learned by doing. Once a geography teacher, now he knows more about the geography of the human mind.'

Raymond To himself is 'very Hong Kong' and once said that he slowed down so much when he was in New York (on a playwriting grant) that 'I thought I was getting sick. When I keep calm and slow down, I get nervous and have to take tranquillizers. In 1993 when I returned to Hong Kong, I came on to the beat of the Hong Kong people. My head beat quicker.'

Film and Theatre: Struggle or Embrace?

There are and have been three basic forms of professional theatre in Hong Kong. These are spoken or 'realistic' drama and the two popular opera forms, Peking and Cantonese. And perhaps no form of live theatre was ever so wedded to commercial cinema as was Cantonese opera to Hong Kong films, at least until the 1950s. In the following two decades the masters retired or died, and, with minimal government or public support, Cantonese opera, like Peking opera in China today, became a comatose art – which was surprising, given the flexibility of the form and the way Cantonese opera has so vigorously competed with films, particularly in the 1930s.

Things are better today, with around 600 performances annually, but few writers are interested in writing specifically for Cantonese opera although there is government encouragement to do so. *Mad Phoenix* itself highlights an era when theatre and film entered into an embrace just as passionate as in the current Springtime phenomenon. It tells the intriguing story of the Cantonese playwright and film-maker, Nam Hoi Sap Sam Long (literally, 'Thirteenth Child' from Nam Hoi), who, besides playwriting for famous opera performers like Sit Kok-sin (as discussed later), also directed several films.

For its enjoyment Ko's film version unfortunately requires basic knowledge of Cantonese opera and of the artists involved, who in those days of the 1930s moved freely between writing, producing, and performing dramatic operas and making films, often of those same operas. But even basic knowledge is illuminating, for the real-life figures in the play (dramatized with some

Top: from Daniel S. P. Yang's production of his own translation of *King Lear* for the Hong Kong Rep, with Hu Qinshu as Lear. Bottom: Yang (centre) with the Hong Kong Rep company in rehearsal.

licence) personify the very earliest connections between the stage (especially Cantonese opera) and the film business in Hong Kong.

Sap Sam Long also helped to launch the film career of his talented niece, Mui Yee, star of many films in Hong Kong before and after the war. In 1937, aged seventeen, she used her pocket money to buy a passage from Shanghai to Hong Kong, where a screen test resulted in her first movie, *War and Survival* (1937), written and directed by her 'Mad Phoenix' uncle.

As with many female stars of post-war Hong Kong cinema, Mui's private life ran the full gamut of success and tragedy. Like many film artists, she was initially trapped in Hong Kong when the Japanese overran Kowloon in December 1941, but with her then-husband, the actor Cheung Ying, fled first via Macau to 'Canton Bay' (adjoining Guangsai province and nominally under French control), then to Kweilin, which remained free of Japanese control throughout the war. Mui, who died in 1966, is also a character in *Mad Phoenix.*

Although Cantonese opera is 'healthier' in Hong Kong than it is in the neighbouring, Cantonese-speaking Guangdong, there are only five local writers working in the form, according to one of them, Bernice Au Man-fbng. In October last year, Ms Au had a half-hour work performed in the foyer of the Hong Kong Cultural Centre. She is young – which is unusual and important for this form, if it is to rise out of its creative doldrums – and Cantonese opera appears to be her lifetime commitment.

Clearly, there is nothing of the 'fixedness' of Peking opera in its Cantonese cousin, which, according to Ms Au, a passionate researcher, first came to Hong Kong in about 1890. Cantonese opera has always absorbed foreign influences, and, as the film historian Law Kar notes, 'It has changed considerably since the nineteenth century, absorbing some facets of Peking opera like the stylized *kung fu.*'

The pre-war years were richly creative, and when Cantonese opera had to compete with Cantonese talkies after 1933 it did so vigorously, with its plots from Hollywood films, contemporary dress, western music such as jazz, and even sexy bubble baths onstage. If a 'live' gimmick could compete with the cinema, it could go into Cantonese opera.

As an example of its 'contemporaneity', in the late 1940s Cantonese opera portrayed Mahatma Gandhi in *Gandhi Dreaming of Shi Shi*, a love story involving the great Indian patriot and (in his dream) Shi Shi, one of the great beauties of Chinese history – also a great patriot for the state of Viet during the period of the Warring States in China.

According to Law Kar, *two* first Cantonese talkies were made almost simultaneously in 1933 – neither of them in Hong Kong, though both can be justified as 'Hong Kong' films, and both were adapted from Cantonese operas. One of these, *The Platinum*

Dragon (*Bai Jinlong*, 1933), was an adaptation from a famous opera written and performed by Sit Kok-sin, and further adapted from a film starring Adolphe Menjou. Sit was almost to Cantonese Opera what the great Mei Lanfang was to Peking opera, although he had strong competition from Ma Tse-tsang – who was also recruited into films and who also injected his love for Hollywood into his operas.

The Platinum Dragon was extremely popular in all the Chinese communities of Guangzhou, Hong Kong, Nanyang (South East Asia), as well as on the West Coast of the United States – Sit and Ma Tse-tsang both having assimilated western, local, and northern (Peking) influences. (Overseas Chinese communities played an important part in sustaining Cantonese opera in the 1920s and 1930s, and were also important to post-war Hong Kong cinema thanks to the distribution networks pioneered by Shaw Bros, as *Tianyi* or, later, *Nanyang*, during the 1930s.)

Romance of the Songsters, the second film identified by Law Kar,[12] was made in San Francisco in 1933-34 by the Grandview Film Company. It starred Kwan Tak-hing, who was then touring the West Coast with his Cantonese opera troupe. Grandview was to function as the Hong Kong cinema in exile when the Japanese occupied the colony from December 1941 to 1945.

Beautiful Kung Fu

Most of Hong Kong's renowned martial artists for the cinema were either trained or influenced by certain opera 'schools'. Even the 'beautiful movements' of John Woo's screen violence make an indirect nod to Cantonese opera as well as to the director's love for Gene Kelly films and for classic cartoons. Jackie Chan and Sammo Hung were rigorously trained in Peking Opera.

Woo's *Princess Chang Ping* (1976) was his 'remake' of *Tragedy of the Emperor's Daughter* (1959), one of *nine* opera films produced in 1959 alone which starred Cantonese opera supremos Yam Kim-fai and Pak Suet-sin, collectively known as 'Yam-Pak'. Historian Law Kar says of these women: 'They are the ones who made Cantonese opera like

Chinese classic literature – but only this troupe [in the post-war years] was so distinguished.' The critic Paul Fonoroff agrees, calling 'several' of their 1959 films 'bona fide classics'.[13] Yam-Pak often collaborated with Tong Dik-sang, almost universally acknowledged as Cantonese opera's finest post-war librettist – and an important character in *Mad Phoenix*.

Yam-Pak were also distinguished in their detailed attention to settings, and to lighting and costume design. They greatly inspired the film-maker Stanley Kwan (*Centre Stage, Rouge*), who often saw them perform when he was a child. In 1996 the Urban Council hired Kwan to direct a prestige presentation of a Cantonese opera called *Till the Sea Runs Dry* to give it the sort of 'look' – in lighting, design, clean sound, etc. – that Yam-Pak might have done.[14] (There is usually no 'director' as such in Cantonese opera, the production often being 'led' by the main performer, working largely to pre-set movements on stage; so hiring a director such as Kwan to add sheen went against tradition.)

Bruce Lee's connection was more indirect. His father, Lee Hoi-chuen, was one of the four major exponents of the 'comedian' role in Cantonese opera during the 1930s. Touring the American West Coast in the late 1930s, the elder Lee married a Eurasian woman – and Bruce Lee was born in 1940. He began an active film career in Hong Kong from the age of ten, though his first leading role was in *The Orphan* (1960), a famous 'lost' film until the colour negative turned up at London's Rank Film Laboratory in 1994.

Bruce was a street fighter who did *kung fu* training in his teens but, after *The Orphan*, his parents – worried about gang reprisals – sent him to the US for a college education. The rest is the stuff of Lee's many biographies. Bruce naturally moved in his father's opera circles, and no doubt imbibed some of their stage fighting techniques.

The Immortal 'Sifu'

Kwan Tak-hing, the star of *Romance of the Songsters*, became a giant of Hong Kong's

Kwan Tak-hing, giant of the post-war cinema, here in one of his many roles as the Cantonese folk hero (and opera star), Huang Fei-hung.

post-war cinema, primarily as the actor who immortalized the Cantonese folk hero Wong Fei Hung (Huang Fei-hung) in films directed by Wu Pang. Little is known about Wong Fei Hung (d. 1924), a righteous figure who – says writer Ng Ho – ran an 'apothecary-cum-martial academy' in Guangzhou. Wong was also the 'chief instructor of the Guangzhou civilian troop, a local patrol organization which arose due to the lack of law and order under the late Qing regime'. Kwan (d. 1995) played the legendary figure in 77 features – 25 of them in 1956 alone. The character has attracted other actors like Jackie Chan (in *Drunken Raster*) and Jet Li (in *Once Upon a Time in China*).

Kwan Tak-hing came directly out of Cantonese opera, which he learned as a child in South-East Asia. His Wong Fei Hung films pioneered the use of real martial arts on screen, and Kwan himself learned the real techniques to became a genuine *sifu*, or master. Like so many of his early contemporaries, he adored Hollywood movies, particularly westerns, and he learned kicks with the whip in America. He was fond of sporting cowboy outfits even into his seventies and eighties. Kwan was also a real-life hero to many Chinese during the Sino-Japanese War (1937–45) – not as a soldier, but through his intensive patriotic work in America and his continuous tours to the front lines in China during the war.[15]

While this article is not concerned with expatriate or touring shows in Hong Kong, it is worth mentioning that a tiny piece of John Bull's Island remains in the professional Punchline Comedy Club, run by John Moorhead. Moorhead brings in at least two top comedians, usually from the UK, for four performances monthly at the Viceroy, in Wan Chai. Always packed, it feels like any busy venue in London and is likely to remain that way well into the future.

Secondly, professional touring shows to Hong Kong started early. Records show that the first theatrical company to visit Hong Kong was from Australia 'as early as 1842', when they paid 'this still somewhat barren island a visit, doing much to enliven the winter evenings.' Next winter came 'a slightly better type of company . . . under a sino Delle Casse. They must have found the tour worth while, as they continued to occupy the theatre until 1844.'[16]

Notes and References

1. Later that year, Maggie Cheung earned the first of several 'best actress' statuettes for her role as the Shanghai screen legend, Ruan Lingyu, in Stanley Kwan's film, *Centre Stage*. Leslie Cheung, memorable in films like *A Better Tomorrow* (dir. John Woo) and *Rouge* (dir. Stanley Kwan), was making a 'comeback' after a brief retirement to Canada. He would soon earn international acclaim for his work in Chen Kaige's *Farewell My Concubine*, joint winner with Jane Campion's *The Piano* of the Cannes Palme d'Or. As Stephen Chow's recent films were consistently outgrossing all others (including Jackie Chan's), perhaps his presence in the film made it doubly 'hot'.

2. Or 'heroic bloodshed' films, an action sub-genre primarily identified with Woo.

3. From Hong Kong's first feature in 1913 to 30 June 1996, 8,500 features had been produced in Hong Kong,

almost 8,000 since the Second World War. Other complex developments included competiton between the Mandarin and Cantonese-language industries (the former largely from Shanghai emigrés) from as early as the mid-1930s.

4. Since the late 1970s, the Hong Kong International Film Festival has rescreened several of these films in the festival's important retrospective programmes under various theme headings – swordplay films, Cantonese melodrama, etc. Until recently, the catalogues of these retrospectives provided the only comprehensive research materials in English on these films, which were rarely studied, or even mentioned in 'world' cinema encyclopedias.

5. *I Have a Date with Spring*, by Raymond To, was first staged by the Hong Kong Repertory Theatre at City Hall Theatre, Hong Kong, from 16 to 31 October 1992. Revivals were staged at the Sai Wan Ho Civic Centre Theatre in Hong Kong from 17 to 23 June 1993, and at the Tsuen Wan Town Hall auditorium, Kowloon, from 2 to 4 July 1993.

6. This is from my viewings of the film. I did not see the stage version. I did see both screen and stage versions of *Mad Phoenix* – the former being extremely faithful to the latter.

7. Both for their roles in this film – Alice Lau as 'best newcomer' and Lo Koon-lan as 'best supporting actress' – at the Hong Kong Film Awards for 1995.

8. This short feature was co-produced by the American, Benjamin Brodsky, and three Hong Kong film-makers – including Li Menwei, the 'father of Hong Kong cinema'.

9. A ballroom-dancing story which was a cult hit in the USA in 1997.

10. *The Legend of the Mad Phoenix* was originally staged by the Hong Kong Repertory Theatre for sixteen performances at the Sai Wan Ho Civic Centre theatre from 28 October to 9 November 1992. Revivals were staged from 11 to 15 January 1995 and at Shatin Town Hall from 20 to 22 January 1995. The 1997 film – and the restaged play – reduced the title to *Mad Phoenix*.

11. Hong Kong became an 'SAR' (Special Administrative Region) of China from 1 July 1997.

12. Law Kar delivered a paper in October 1997 on the subject of the American–Hong Kong Film Connection, at a conference on Hong Kong cinema at the University of Illinois in Urbana–Champaign.

13. Fonoroff's book, *Silver Light: a Pictorial History of Hong Kong Cinema, 1920–1970* (Hong Kong: Joint Publishing, 1997), is one of the best recent studies of Hong Kong cinema. Fonoroff is a long-time critic of Chinese and Hong Kong cinema, occasionally 'guesting' in foreigner roles in Hong Kong films.

14. There were four performances at the Grand Theatre, Hong Kong Cultural Centre, from 16 to 18 May 1997.

15. In August 1942, the South China Motion Picture Performers' Federation had 'four plays under production, two in Mandarin and two in Cantonese'. This was in Hong Kong under Japanese occupation. One of the plays, written by Cho Yu, had 'some time ago' had a 'record run of 26 days in one theatre' – as reported in the *Hongkong News* (then Hong Kong's only English-language daily, run by Japanese business interests) on 22 August 1942.

16. See V. H. G. Jarrett, *Old Hong Kong* (1934), Public Records Office, Hong Kong.

Gay McAuley

Towards an Ethnography of Rehearsal

Twenty-five years ago, the original *Theatre Quarterly* pioneered the documentation of the rehearsal process in a series of 'Production Casebooks' which, in a wide variety of formats – dictated by the people and the facilities available for any particular production – delved pragmatically into then-uncharted territory. That such analyses are now more commonplace is thanks not only to the active participation of academics in the field of theatre studies, but also to what Gay McAuley here describes as the postmodern 'shift in interest from the reified art object to the dynamic processes involved in its production and reception'. But the need to refine happenstance into methodology has served only to highlight the problems of observation, selection, and presentation involved – and of how to determine the degree of objectivity that is possible or desirable. The availability of video alongside audiotape and notebook provides an important additional tool – but presents its own problems of 'editing' and interpretation. Here, Gay McAuley, Director of the Centre for Performance Studies in the University of Sydney, compares the dilemma of the rehearsal recordist with that of the cultural anthropologist, and proposes the value of an ethnographic model in recognizing and starting to embrace if not always to overcome the difficulties which confront the involved observer. An earlier version of her paper was read at the IFTR/FIRT conference 'Actor, Actress on Stage', held in Montreal in June 1995.

THE DESIRE TO OBSERVE and analyze rehearsals is probably a peculiarly modern (or, rather, postmodern) phenomenon, born of the shift in interest from the reified art object to the dynamic processes involved in its production and reception. Theatre practitioners have traditionally regarded the rehearsal period as private: they rarely admit outsiders or observers, and even more rarely have practitioners themselves documented the rehearsal process in any detail. The historical record is, therefore, very thin, and I do not know of any detailed account of a rehearsal process before the twentieth-century rise of the director as the dominant artist in the production process.

Certain directors, however, have shown an interest in documenting their own creative process. While Stanislavsky's written *mises en scène* for plays like *The Seagull* and *Othello*[1] do not document the rehearsal process, they do give some insight into his working method, and later directors such as Peter Brook, Max Stafford-Clark and John Dexter[2] have either published casebooks or diary accounts of their work on a particular production or have authorised other writers

to do so. In these accounts it is, understandably, the work of the director that is foregrounded, and this is also the case in the studies by academics that are beginning to appear.[3] Actors' memoirs frequently contain fascinating, albeit fragmentary, references to rehearsal experiences but it is very rare for an actor to publish a detailed account of his/her work on a particular production.[4]

At the Centre for Performance Studies at the University of Sydney, we are developing a range of methods for the study of performance, and an important part of this has been the attempt to document and analyze rehearsal process. While it remains very difficult to gain access to rehearsals in the professional theatre for academic or student observers, we have been observing and documenting the rehearsal process in all the professional workshop productions that we have sponsored over the last ten years. This paper addresses some of the methodological and ethical issues raised by this work.

Our recording technique has changed over the years that we have been experimenting: in the beginning we simply had academic observers in the rehearsal room, watching and taking notes; later we began to use a tape recorder and to transcribe some of the rehearsal room discussions as part of subsequent analyses; then we used a video camera set up in a corner of the room and left running throughout the process; and most recently we have had two cameras, one taking a generalized wide shot, the other manned by an operator who can record more detail of facial expression, etc.

Processes and Privileging

Each of these methods of recording and documenting tends to privilege different aspects of the process; each reveals certain attitudes to both the rehearsal process and the analytical enterprise – and indeed the subsequent analyses will be strongly marked by the perceptual framework constructed by the chosen method of documentation. Recordings cannot, of course, replace the live presence of the academic observer, but they have proved to be a very effective supplement to memory and note-taking, and they can serve as a valuable corrective to interpretive views that may develop during the analytical phase, as long as one maintains an appropriately critical awareness of the mediating function of the recording methodology adopted.

Video unquestionably provides a much richer record than audio recording, but – certainly in the predominantly western forms of performance I have observed – it has been my experience that rehearsal is a highly verbal activity, and a sound record can therefore be a very useful document. It is always important to have good-quality sound recording, for so much of the creative process is articulated through the questions, explanations, anecdotes, and jokes which abound in the rehearsal room. In a master's thesis concerned with rehearsal,[5] Marion Potts argues that the anecdote is the principal means whereby performance theory is articulated and transmitted from one group to another in this highly oral professional practice.

Jim Sharman, reflecting on his long experience as a director, makes a similar point when he compares theatre practitioners to 'a lost tribe with only an oral tradition handed down erratically from person to person, usually as gossip'.[6] Jokes are equally vital, and can be seen, among other things, as an important part of the actors' strategy for negotiating the interface between their characters' and their own subjectivities.

The dominance of jokes and laughter in the earliest stages of the rehearsal process, notably during the first readings in text-based performance work, and the relative absence of such behaviours later in the process, bear out this analysis of their function. Jokes, gossip, and story-telling, then, can all be seen as important dimensions of the creative process, and what might appear on the surface to be a diversion or distraction may in fact be fulfilling a directly functional role in the work.

One problem with our documentation strategy is the sheer bulk of material that it now produces: one week of rehearsal produces at least thirty hours of videotape, and the material is not easily accessible to users, especially if they were not present at the time. It sometimes seems that we are like the cartographer in the Borges story whose map was so precise and so detailed that it eventually became co-extensive with the territory it mapped.

Any editing or re-working of the recorded material, has, however, always seemed to me to be extremely problematical for both ethical and other reasons. The directors and actors who agree to work in the laboratory-style conditions we provide at the university accept that their work is being recorded, and that the filmed material will be kept in our video archive; but there is a significant distinction for them between documentation and subsequent analysis and interpretation, and the latter raises very delicate questions which can put at risk the whole fragile relationship of trust that is being built up between artists and academics.

It can be argued, of course, that documentation of any sort necessarily involves selection and is, therefore, already in itself a form of analysis or even interpretation. Making a sound recording of a rehearsal indicates an assumption about the importance of the verbal in the process; sitting in the room noting the blocking as it develops reveals assumptions about the function of space as a performance signifier; and so on. While this is true, it must be acknowledged that analysis, whether it takes the form of a written document or an edited film, involves a much more intrusive kind of interpretation, a far more obvious ordering and shaping of the material.

Lessons from Ethnography?

The documentation and analysis of rehearsal process has much in common with the work of the field ethnographer, and it seems to me that in our practice of observing and recording rehearsals at the University of Sydney we have followed, albeit unconsciously in the early days, the ethnographic model of participant observation, since the academic observer is constantly present in the rehearsal room, *in* it but not *of* it, 'maintaining' (in Margaret Mead's telling phrase) 'the balance between empathic involvement and disciplined detachment'.[7]

Hélène Bouvier, discussing the aspects of anthropological method which are the most valuable for theatre studies, also singles out this dual strategy of 'immersion in another community or society' and the 'purposeful distancing in time and space (rivalling with the empathy generated by field presence)'.[8]

Anthropology has traditionally taken as its object of study societies and cultures far removed from that of the anthropologist, and in the application of anthropological method to domains such as theatre studies the tendency to date has been to shift the focus of attention from western theatre to the performance traditions of other cultures or to a range of intercultural practices.[9] Valuable as this opening of the perspective has been, it seems to me that it can be equally valuable to apply the methods of anthropology to the theatre practices of our own culture, to begin the study of the 'other' within our midst.

There are many similarities between the situation of ethnographers in the field and academic observers in the rehearsal room. The latter, like the former, can be positioned by their hosts (some directors, alarmed at the potentially disruptive impact of an observer, may require that the observer fulfil some task in the process, become part of the process in an overt way); rehearsal analysts, like ethnographers, may be shown what their hosts think they want to see, or what the group think they should see (a performance of rehearsal rather than a genuine rehearsal); or they may be shown only what it is thought appropriate to show to an outsider (Susan Letzler Cole was asked to leave a rehearsal of the Wooster Group's *Saint Anthony* at a particularly fraught moment, even after she had been attending rehearsals for some weeks,[10] and there have been occasions in work I have documented when student observers have been asked to leave).

These comments make clear that the relationship between observer and observed involves complex and subtle issues of power and presence, and ethnographic practice has much to teach us about the observation phase in such work. My focus in this paper is, however, predominantly on the next phase – the writing up and presentation of analysis based on the experience, and it is here that the developing discipline of performance studies has most to learn from current thinking in anthropology. Indeed, the very notion of phases, the valorization of the analysis that follows immersion in the field experience, is one of the first lessons that the theatre specialist can learn from ethnography.

In theatre studies, the productions that form part of our research and teaching all too often do not lead to extended study, but make of us pseudo-practitioners, caught up in the unceasing need to produce more theatre, denying ourselves the space for reflection and analysis. Ethnographic practice provides a useful alternative model: a period spent in the field followed by many months (even years) of study, reflection, and writing: for fieldwork must be 'written up', the film shot in the field must be edited, subjected to the shaping and ordering process that turns it into an object of knowledge.

When I began observing and documenting rehearsal, I used my records essentially as a means of tracking back to find the genesis of key performance decisions: that is to say, I was essentially product- rather than process-orientated, and was using the rehearsal material primarily for the light it shed on the performance object. Like the practitioners, perhaps, I saw rehearsal as a means to an end and my interest was in the performance rather than in the production process as a subject of study in itself.

The Product and the Process

The shift of interest from art object to the process of production, already mentioned as characteristic of this postmodern moment, is given a methodological basis through the interface with ethnography. Possibly even more valuable is the practice now being developed in ethnography whereby, in a third phase of the work, the ethnographer returns to the field with the edited film record of the earlier visit, shows it to the original informants and others, and records their responses. The reportage/analysis thus becomes an element in a communicative process, able to be presented to those it most closely concerns, who were excluded from the analytical process in traditional anthropology, and then possibly recast in the light of their responses.

Recent articles on ethnography[11] have thus made me realize that our attempts at neutral and unobtrusive recording, our refusal to edit these recordings in any way, and the ways in which we have been using our partial analyses are less the high-minded attempt to meet the artists' legitimate demands that we considered them to be than a failure to grapple honestly with the analytical enterprise and the power relations it necessarily entails.

Kirsten Hastrup, writing movingly about the violence inherent in ethnographic practice, concludes that, none the less, 'There is no way to evade the burden of authorship, however heavy it has become',[12] and I would argue that it is essentially through the constraints on analysis imposed by the reporting-back phase, and the alternative views produced through the feedback, that the issues of power can be addressed.

The immediate trigger for this paper was the experience of attempting to edit the raw footage of rehearsal documentation into an 'ethnographic'-style film. I had hoped that the film would be finished before I wrote the paper but, for budgetary reasons that will be familiar to all university researchers nowadays, the editing process is taking much longer than anticipated, so my remarks concern only my own response to what I have learned (what I am learning).

In a third phase of the work, for the reasons outlined above, I will show the film to the director and actors involved in the production, and record their responses. This third phase is crucial, for the point of the exercise is not just for me to say through the film 'this is what happened' – we all appreciate today that there can be many versions of 'what happened', and that many stories can be told with the same footage. The ethnographic model suggests, however, that until I try to say 'this is what I saw' I have not understood what I saw. As Solveig Freudenthal puts it, we need to 'both see and understand an event',[13] thus making it clear that seeing is not synonymous with understanding.

Film brings with it a certain risk of closure; people can see the film who were not present at the rehearsal; film exists in the present when the original experience is only a memory; film tends over time to replace even the memory. All these are further reasons why the feedback aspect of the project is so important: the film is not intended to be the final word, but a means of producing dialogue. What follows are some general reflections emerging from the first two phases of this project, and also from my experience as a participant observer in the rehearsal process over a number of years.

Any attempt to record the rehearsal process raises the immediate questions of when and where to begin and what to include. As Timothy Asch points out, 'Observers and subjects may differ greatly in their perceptions of when an event or interaction begins and ends and whom it includes',[14] and theatrical production is an extraordinarily diffuse process that can occur over a long period of time and involve a large number of different individuals working in different locations and in different media.

Antony Sher's account of his work on Richard III shows that he began thinking and dreaming about the part and consciously noting physical possibilities for an interpretation months before he even knew with certainty that he would play the part. By the time the rehearsals began he had already done an enormous amount of work.

The Bounded Nature of the Event

It is certainly true that many important creative decisions have been made before the actors meet for the first time in the rehearsal room, and many factors that will have a significant bearing on the final outcome will already have been introduced: the director's work on the text (if there is one), the formulation of the project for presentation to funding authorities, the casting process itself, the discussions between the director and the actors during the casting, between director and agents, and between actors and agents could all legitimately be seen as part of the rehearsal process.

The custom, regrettably all too widespread nowadays, of having set and costumes designed before the actors have begun their work means that many of their creative decisions have effectively been pre-empted before the rehearsals proper begin; whatever one thinks about a production system that subordinates the actor to the designer, it is evident that the design process, whenever and wherever it occurs, is an important part of the construction of meaning and needs to be documented and included in the account.

Even if, for the purposes of video documentation, it is agreed that the rehearsal process will be defined as that which takes place once the actors, director, and production team come together for the first time in the rehearsal room, there are still questions about what to record. It is my experience that very informative discussions can occur in the coffee breaks, over lunch, and also in the dressing rooms. Sometimes key performance decisions emerge from ideas which were first articulated in one of these marginal spaces in the process. In the last two productions I observed, a small number of nicotine-dependent participants would regularly go outside for a smoke and, again, the discussions amongst the 'smokers' group' were so germane to the whole process that we regretted not having another camera available.

There are no clear answers to the question of defining the boundaries of rehearsal, but the very task of documentation prompts some interesting questions that might otherwise not be raised. Bringing an outsider's eye to the insiders' world of rehearsal (the classic ethnographic situation) can be revealing both for outsiders and insiders.

Does the presence of an observer during the rehearsal process necessarily, by his or her very presence, transform the event? If so, does this then render invalid the observations made by such a person? Is there a sense in which the 'real' rehearsal process is always tantalizingly beyond the reach of the academic analyst? Some practitioners may say yes to all three questions, and certainly those directors who create an artificial job for the observer – masking his presence as outsider and turning him into a pseudo-insider – clearly fear the potential transformation that an observer might cause.

Critical theorists would agree that the event is affected, even transformed by the presence of an observer, but, rather than bewailing the impossibility of objective knowledge of an ideal reality, would point out that all knowledge is necessarily mediated and always has been, even though it is only in recent years that we have begun to recognize this. In response to this kind of thinking, anthropologists have begun to question their earlier beliefs concerning the 'transparency of representation and the immediacy of experience',[15] and to consider the methodological implications of such a conceptual shift.

Kirsten Hastrup bases her ethnographic work on the recognition that anthropologists in the field are dealing 'not with the un-mediated world of the "others" but the world between ourselves and the others', and she accepts that the 'knowledge produced is doubly mediated by our own presence, and the informant's response to that'.[16] Exactly the same can be said of the situation of the observer/analyst in the rehearsal.

The Observer and the 'Native Ethnographer'

The fact that there is no such person as a neutral or transparent observer, and that any analysis and even any description will bear the imprint of its own cultural moment, does not, however, invalidate the record. Readers of the record will also be reading from within their own cultural moment, as readers of all sorts have always done, and understanding is an ongoing, always incomplete process.

Acknowledging as inevitable that the observer's presence will change the event does not, of course, remove the practical obligation to be as unobtrusive as possible. We have tried to minimize the impact of the recording apparatus in our projects, and observers have learned to exercise tact and discretion about where to sit in the space, when to ask questions, when (if at all) to volunteer information.

What is important, however, is both to acknowledge and to be sensitive to the mediations that are occurring. Theatre practitioners may welcome the interest shown in their work process, or they may perceive the presence of an academic observer to be an irritation, tending to increase the stress levels (hence the tendency to ask observers to leave the rehearsal if relations between participants are becoming severely strained), or the scholar's presumed knowledge may be felt as a kind of threat, or any combination of these.

Actors in one of our projects (which was observed by three academics) told us that they were frequently mystified as to what triggered us all to write notes at certain moments, and in that case as in many others the observers themselves were certainly being observed. The practitioners work from within institutional and cultural frameworks that predispose them to see the observer in certain ways. The academy – place of critical, analytical, and theoretical discourse – has traditionally been regarded with suspicion if not hostility by theatre artists, and, as I have already indicated, the academic observer is likely to be positioned more or less overtly by the practitioners, may be given a part to play within the process, may be more or less consciously excluded from certain aspects of the work, may even be asked to leave the room on occasion.

But observers, too, observe from within certain institutional and cultural frameworks, and see primarily what these frameworks allow them to see. This, however, only becomes apparent when the analysis is written up and the analyst attempts to transform seeing into understanding. Furthermore, it will only be when we have available a good number of descriptive analyses, undertaken over a number of years, that we will be able to begin to recognize the impact of the analysts' conceptual frameworks, institutional constraints, and so on.

The contemporary ethnographic model posits an outsider immersing himself in the culture of the insiders, reporting back both to his own society about the culture he has observed and to the insiders, opening up the space of a dialogue between the two. In recent years another idea, that of the 'native ethnographer', of insiders reporting on their own culture, has gained more currency, and this raises a very important methodological issue in terms of rehearsal analysis. Should the observation, documentation and analysis of rehearsal process be undertaken by the artists themselves? Is this possible? Is it in fact preferable to the outside participant observer model I have been developing?

James Clifford makes the valid point that 'Insiders studying their own cultures offer new angles of vision and depths of understanding', but adds an important rider: 'their accounts are empowered and restricted in unique ways'.[17] There are questions of power involved with both insider and outsider accounts. Who has the right to tell the tale? Who sees more of what is going on?

Who is the more and who is the less institutionally constrained in the seeing and in the telling? (It is worth stressing again that seeing and telling are no more synonymous than seeing and understanding).

There is a small practical point to be made here, but it has important strategic implications: observation is, in my experience, a full-time role which precludes even taking responsibility for sound recording or camera operation, so I would suggest that there are serious methodological problems for someone who has a major creative involvement with the production also attempting to observe and analyze the whole of the process.

Accounts by artists of their own experience in the productive process are of course invaluable, as I have already indicated in relation to published accounts by artists like Max Stafford-Clark and Antony Sher. These are, however, a different kind of undertaking from the descriptive analysis of the whole process, have a different kind of 'truth value', and a different (though utterly crucial) role to play in our developing theoretical appreciation of the creative processes involved.

Point-of-View in the Analysis

The first problem confronting anyone who is attempting to present or analyze rehearsal process is that of the narrative framework. There is no way to present the process, whether in print or on film, without transforming it into a story of some kind and, as we have all been made aware by the critical theorists, there is no such thing as a neutral frame or a story without point-of-view. Whatever narrative point of view is adopted is inevitably going to influence the interpretation and colour the analysis.

The first option I considered when beginning to edit the thirty hours of film in my pilot project was the diary format, which respects the chronological order of events. Chronological order and third-person narration certainly provide a comforting sense of objectivity, but the editing process makes it abundantly clear that this apparent objectivity is simply a mask for one's own involvement.

Even with the alibi of chronology, it is still the analyst/film maker who must select the events and determine how much of any interaction to include. A film structured in this way would still be my story and I would be the subject of its enunciation. Of course, I could mask my presence by using graphic inserts rather than voice-over for the narrative links, but the film medium also permits me to acknowledge it openly by using my own voice for these and for any commentary.

Another possibility was to begin from the end – that is, begin with the performance produced by the process, and work back to show how it was generated. This format requires a great deal more interpretive analysis and editorial intervention than the chronological account, and an almost inevitable consequence is that explorations that were not ultimately included in the production will be set aside, seen as red herrings, or minimized. The major impact of such a format is that it will show the process to have been essentially goal-oriented and instrumental, where this might or might not have been the case.

Another possibility was to tell the story from the director's point of view. The film could even become the director's account of her own process: I could consult her on the selection of material to include, interview her, and then edit that material as voice-over commentary in her own voice, or ask her to script and record her own commentary to provide the narrative links. In this case the reporting back phase would involve the actors, designer, and other creative agents, but not the director.

Or it could be told from the actors' point of view But *one* of the actors? Which one? All of them? Involving all the actors would be extremely difficult logistically and technically, but choosing to privilege one would obviously be a very loaded decision.

What this preliminary phase made abundantly clear was that there is no obviously correct way to present the material, and that one has to be alert to the implications of whatever narrative format one does adopt, for any telling is necessarily an interpretation. There is another point that needs to be teased out here: even if I think I am telling the story from the director's or from a given actor's point of view, even if the commentary is in their own voice, it is still my analytical enterprise, and I am inserting the actors' and the director's stories into another, larger narrative.

In the case of the pilot project this master narrative is still taking shape, but I do already know that here, too, there are several possibilities: I can tell a story of communal effort towards a shared goal in which all the strategies employed in the rehearsal are validated by this common purpose, but I could also tell a more sinister tale of female subjectivities being disciplined in order that a male story can be unproblematically reproduced (a frequent occurrence when plays from the classical repertoire are involved), or one of actors' subjectivities being subdued in order to serve a director's vision.

Edited Film or Written Account?

My decision to edit the video recording of rehearsal was made in part due to my disquiet about the sheer bulk of the material we have been producing, and what might be called its opaqueness as a document to all save those who were present during the project in question. The decision does, however, immediately raise questions about the nature of film and about the relative merits of film and written account as vehicles for description and analysis.

The principal value of film in this kind of reportage is, as Solveig Freudenthal has expressed it, that it 'enables us to experience, as no other medium can, the "all-at-once-ness" or what Geertz has called the thickness of social life', and that 'the camera permits us to confront the compoundedness of activities'.[18] Ethnographers have discovered that it is, however, not the most appropriate vehicle for analytical discourse, nor even for the explanatory background material that will enable viewers to make sense of what they see. Timothy Asch puts it succinctly:

When filmmakers try to provide extensive background through narration they obscure what film can do; that is, they tend to obliterate what is being conveyed by the subjects' actions and speech.[19]

Most ethnographers who use film would agree that both film and verbal analysis (written or spoken) are required, and indeed it is customary in many places for the showing of an ethnographic film to be situated within the context of a lecture or other academic presentation. This is also increasingly the case in theatre studies, where in teaching situations and in scholarly conferences, extracts from video recordings are routinely used to illustrate points or to serve as stand-in for the absent performance.

In ethnographic practice, film is frequently (normally?) placed within a larger, predominantly verbal, discourse which tends to obviate the necessity for analytical and explanatory material to be incorporated within it, and thus serves principally to illustrate the analysis that is being made verbally. This practice, while offering the attractions of flexibility to the analyst, needs to be approached with some caution and with an awareness of the ethical responsibility of the analyst towards both the filmmaker (if this is a different person) as well as towards the subjects of the film.

The film in these circumstances is experienced by the viewer through the filter of the verbal analysis in which it is embedded; fragments only of the filmed experience may be shown, and the subjects of the film have no control over this kind of editing and filtering. It seems to me that in the developing discipline of theatre and performance studies we need to think much more critically about the ways in which we are using video, and this is even more important when the subject of the recording is the rehearsal (something the participants regard as private), rather than the finished performance (which is already in a certain sense in the public domain).

All too often in our conferences and lectures the provenance of the video recordings that are shown is unstated: they are presented as though they do indeed 'stand for' the performance. Thus the choices made by film-maker and editor, the impact these may have on interpretation, and even the analyst's role in the film-making, are not discussed.

The reader of a written description of rehearsal, unsupplemented by film, is totally dependent on the writer, sees through the writer's eyes, sees only what the writer describes, and must experience the event in the order in which the writer tells it. Film, as has already been pointed out, provides the opportunity for analysts to speak in their own voice in the narrative links, or to mask this with a voice-over in another voice, or with graphic inserts which approach the apparent objective authority of written text. One of the most valuable attributes of film in this kind of work is that the medium itself imposes a degree of self-reflexivity, choices have to be made, and authorial voice becomes a problematic category.

Complexities of Filmic Mediation

Readers have to interpret what they read and, as the reception theorists have shown, the meanings readers construct may not be those intended by the writer, but it is none the less clear that ethnographic film leaves open more opportunities for interpretation than written text. Written descriptions are more tightly connected to the writer's interpretation of the event, but film provides a great deal of information which may in fact undercut the analysis that the ethnographer makes of the events filmed, and the value of film is that it is still there twenty, thirty, or fifty years later (but perhaps not indefinitely), ready to be re-viewed, re-interpreted in the light of different intellectual and ideological agendas. The closure effected by film in its ability to supplant the events filmed is paradoxically countered by this very longevity: film outlives even the analyses it facilitates.

It is of course true that film is also a highly focused, selective recording medium, not only due to the mediating function of the camera, but also to the whole film process (editing, montage, voice-over narration,

etc). However carefully the film is made, we must recognize that we are necessarily dealing with multiple layers of meaning-making and interpretation, which include the views of the subjects within the process which have been incorporated in one form or another in the film; those of the academic analyst whose interpretation guides the editing; and the impact of the film process itself (the choice of one shot rather than another will often be made on film aesthetic grounds rather than in terms of the rehearsal activity). Then, of course, the film is necessarily interpreted by its viewers in terms of their ideologies and institutional frameworks.

A brief anecdote will illustrate the complexities in play here: in one of our projects, involving two actors and a director working on the murder scene in *Othello*, the director set a rehearsal exercise in which she and the actor playing Othello stood on either side of the actress playing Desdemona and whispered into her ears all the vile accusations that are made about Desdemona in the play. The actress could reply only with the few words Shakespeare has chosen to give to Desdemona in that scene.

This went on and on remorselessly, the pathos of her protestations of innocence becoming more and more desperate in the face of the paranoid violence encasing her. Eventually the actress broke down and wept, really wept for about three minutes. My colleague Terry Threadgold, who was present with me in the rehearsal room, and was as deeply moved as I was by the exercise, has used it in an analysis of the way that masculine and feminine subjectivities are constructed in society, how women are led to a state of 'internalized and unconscious compliance with the structures of the patriarchal order'.[20]

When she presented her analysis of the process some time later to students who had not themselves observed the rehearsals, nor seen the final performance, many were disturbed at the tactic employed in the rehearsal exercise, some even feeling that, as observers we had been part of the violence employed. The video camera had focused on the actress's face throughout the whole scene, and it seemed to me, in comparing my memory of the event with the video record, that the film process itself had to an extent falsified what occurred.

My memory was that all the women in the room were deeply moved, and that what was happening in the rehearsal was not an act of brutality towards the actress, but a powerful moment of shared grieving, involving for each of us a complex mix of personal experience, our knowledge of the situation of women in our society, and the dramatic situation Shakespeare had crafted.

This example illustrates how the verbal discourse in which a filmed record may be situated and the way an interaction is filmed both become part of the meaning for later viewers. Thus, the most apparently neutral camera position (the camera in the *Othello* project was situated at the back of the room and during the exercise in question had, I believe, been forgotten by everyone present, except the operator, who was himself deeply moved) is capable of conveying a far from neutral message, for conventions prevailing in the cinema predispose viewers to read shots in certain ways (in this example the focus on the actress's face, the unmoving camera, and the duration of the shot contributed to perceptions of the film as 'intrusive', 'merciless', and 'painful').

The main point I want to make with this anecdote is that there is no final 'truth' to be told or extracted from the account of any rehearsal, only a more and more profound appreciation of the complexity of the processes involved. More importantly still, the example suggests how valuable it is that a number of analysts should be working on the same material when there are multiple points of view in the analysis (and this is something that does not happen very often in ethnographic fieldwork). For while no-one knows 'the' truth, multiple analyses will reveal multiple partial truths (in the double sense in which James Clifford uses the term), and the more of these partial analyses we can have of a given process, the more we will appreciate how partial each one is.

Modern ethnographic practice is posited on what Jean-Paul Dumont calls the 'back and forth movement between experience and consciousness',[21] and in contemporary ethnography, as the work of Linda Connor and others reveals, this movement may include a return to the original subjects and the incorporation of their responses in a further stage of analysis.

All of this is equally important in the developing discipline of performance studies. Seeing is not necessarily understanding, experience does not necessarily bring knowledge, and what is needed is indeed a constant back and forth movement between the rehearsal or the performance experience and the attempt to write it down, film it, talk about it, between my experience and that of other people involved in the same process. Such a back and forth movement is also a way to address the power relations involved in the analytical enterprise.

Acknowledgements

I would like to express my gratitude to Linda Connor of the Department of Sociology and Anthropology, University of Newcastle, New South Wales, whose critique of traditional practices in ethnographic film-making opened my eyes to the value for performance studies of the new ethnography, and to Lindy Davies (director), Katrina Foster, and Patrick Dickson and Russell Kiefel (actors) in the *Tartuffe* project around which this analysis revolves.

Notes and References

1. Konstantin Stanislavsky, *Stanislavsky Produces Othello*, trans. Helen Nowack (New York: Theatre Arts Books, 1948); and *The Seagull Produced by Stanislavsky*, trans. David Magarshack, ed. S. D. Balukhaty (New York: Theatre Arts Books, 1952).

2. On Peter Brook see, for example, A. C. H. Smith, *Orghast at Persepolis* (New York: Viking Press, 1972); John Heilpern, *The Conference of the Birds* (New York: Bobbs Merrill, 1977); David Selbourne, *The Making of A Midsummer Night's Dream: an Eyewitness Account of Peter Brook's Production from First Rehearsal to First Night* (London: Methuen, 1982). Max Stafford-Clark documented his own work on *The Recruiting Officer* and *Our Country's Good* in *Letters to George* (London: Nick Hern Books, 1988); and John Dexter's production of *Galileo* is described in Jim Hiley, *Theatre at Work: the Story of the National Theatre's Production of Brecht's Galileo* (London: Routledge, 1981).

3. For instance, Susan Letzler Cole, *Directors in Rehearsal: a Hidden World* (London: Routledge, 1992); Shomit Mitter, *Systems of Rehearsal: Stanislavsky, Brecht, Grotowski, and Brook* (London: Routledge, 1992).

4. Antony Sher's *Year of the King* (London: Chatto, 1985), his diary kept during the year he worked on *Richard III*, is particularly valuable for this very reason.

5. C. M. Potts, *What Empty Space? Text and Space in Australian Mainstream Rehearsal Process*, unpublished M.Phil. thesis, University of Sydney, 1995.

6. Jim Sharman, 'In the Realm of the Imagination', 1995 Rex Cramphorn Memorial Lecture, published in *The Sydney Review*, No. 79 (1995), p.10-12.

7. Margaret Mead, 'The Art and Technology of Fieldwork', in Narall and Cohen, eds., *A Handbook of Method in Cultural Anthropology*.

8. Hélène Bouvier, 'Introduction', *Theatre Research International* (Special Issue: Anthropology and Theatre), XIX, No. 1 (1994).

9. See for example Richard Schechner, *Between Theatre and Anthropology* (University of Pennsylvania Press, 1985); Eugenio Barba, *Beyond the Floating Islands* (New York: Performing Arts Journal Publications, 1986); Patrice Pavis, *Le Théâtre au croisement des cultures* (Paris: Corti, 1990); *La Scène et la terre: questions d'ethnoscénologie* (Paris: Babel Maison des Cultures du Monde, 1996).

10. Susan Letzler Cole, op. cit., p. 115.

11. See notably Linda Connor, 'Third Eye: Some Reflections on Collaboration for Ethnographic Film', in Jack R. Rollwagen, ed., *Anthropological Filmmaking* (Harwood Academic Publishers, 1988), p. 97-110; 'Representing Gender in Ethnographic Film', paper read at Research Seminar, Centre for Performance Studies, University of Sydney, 1994; Patsy Asch, 'Subjects, Images, Voices: Representing Gender in Ethnographic Films', *Visual Anthropology Review*, XI, No. 1 (1995), p. 5-18; Judith Okely and Helen Calloway, eds., *Anthropology and Autobiography* (London: Routledge, 1992); James Clifford and George Marcus, *Writing Culture: Poetics and Politics of Ethnography* (University of California Press, 1986); David MacDougall, 'Whose Story Is It?', *Visual Anthropology Review*, VII, No. 2, p. 2-10.

12. Kirsten Hastrup, 'Writing Ethnography: the State of the Art', in Okely and Calloway, eds., *Anthropology and Autobiography* (London: Routledge, 1992), p. 116-33.

13. Solveig Freudenthal, 'What to Tell and How to Show It: Issues in Anthropological Filmmaking', in Jack Rollwagen, *Anthropological Filmmaking* (Harwood Academic Publishers, 1988), p. 123-34.

14. Timothy Asch, 'Collaboration in Ethnographic Filmmaking: a Personal View', in Jack Rollwagen, op. cit., p. 1-29.

15. James Clifford, op. cit., p. 1-26

16. Kirsten Hastrup, op. cit. p. 116-33.

17. James Clifford, op. cit., p. 1-26.

18. Solveig Freudenthal, op. cit., p. 123-34.

19. Timothy Asch, op. cit., p. 1-29.

20. Terry Threadgold, 'Performing Genre: Violence, the Making of Protected Subjects, and the Discourse of Critical Literacy and Radical Pedagogy', in *Changing English*, I, No. 1, p. 2-31.

21. Jean Paul Dumont, *The Headman and I: Ambiguity and Ambivalence in the Fieldworking Experience* (University of Texas Press, 1978).

NTQ Reports and Announcements

Karen Malpede

Idioms and Identities in Cairo

The Ninth Cairo International Festival
for Experimental Theare and Symposium
on Women's/Feminist Theatre,
1–11 September 1997

CAIRO, host to its Ninth International Festival for Experimental Theatre, is itself an experimental city, where a distinctly Arab secular, progressive tolerance lives side by side with Muslim traditionalism, just as speeding cars and donkey carts share the narrow winding lanes and the pre-recorded calls to prayer broadcast five times a day from the minarets of the elegant medieval mosques become difficult to hear amid the never-ending sounds of honking horns in a city that does not sleep.

In the Khan El Khalili bazaars, the beating mercantile heart of the old Islamic city, discarded plastic bags mix with manure and hay to form the slippery underfoot; tourist kitsch and imitation Calvin Kleins are sold alongside traditional, meticulously crafted silver, brass, appliquéd fabrics and hand-blown glass. And upon the black ribbon of the Nile, neon Coca Cola signs and the reflected lights of luxury high-rise blocks cast their eerie glow.

Theatre spaces all around the city, from the modern marble Opera complex to the inside of a medieval camel-trader's house and the outside of the ancient pyramids at Giza, housed over seventy plays from forty countries, some competing for prizes, others on the fringe, and one Egyptian company, El-Warsha, boycotting the Festival from a theatre tent behind the posh British Council.

Despite the fact that not one play written by a woman was selected by its government for performance at the Festival, a two-day international symposium on 'Experimental Trends in Women's/Feminist Theatre', featuring some two dozen women artists and critics from Europe, Africa, North and South America, was held in the garish mirrored interior of the Al Hambre nightclub penthouse at the Cairo Sheraton hotel. This was followed by a day-long seminar on 'Arabic Theatre: Its Heritage and Future Challenges', at which only men were heard and where translation from the Arabic was not available.

Like the city which is its home, the International Festival was alive with contradictions. Improbably bracketed at one end by the deaths of the English Princess Diana and her Egyptian lover – and of the Albanian ascetic Mother Teresa – at the other by the Catholic of Jewish heritage Madelaine Albright's inability to bang the hard heads of Israeli and Palestinian leaders, the Festival seemed fragile, important, useless, necessary, ridiculous – and remarkable. Just one week later, the German tour bus was fire-bombed.

Invited, all expenses paid, by the Egyptian Ministry of Culture, I was there to speak on the Symposium, the only person from the United States to speak publicly at the Festival, and the only Jew. (Robert Brustein, also Jewish, was the invited American honoree and Holly Hill, also from the US, was a judge.) There was no official entry from the United States, due to the funding crisis in the country and our government's dismissal of the importance of international cultural exchange, and this was a terrible shame, since my public endorsement of the peace process and long-time commitment to self-determination for the Palestinian people caused a stir.

But if Arabs have a wrong idea of many of us, so, surely have we been brainwashed against them. The new 'line in the sand' is being drawn between the Judaeo–Christian and the Islamic worlds, and new conflicts are escalating due to the idiocy of extremists on all sides. For me, therefore, it was a wonderful surprise to fall in love with the gentle inhabitants of exhausting and exhilarating Cairo, to exult not only in the pyramids and strange, compelling beauty of the desert, but to feel, at first hand, the dignity and grace of Cairenes and their Muslim city, and to experience the safety of a crowded public space where people do not mug or steal. In Egypt, I found the people tolerant and warm. I was troubled that so often on the street women in the veil would not look me in the eyes; but I also was able to speak as friends with veiled women at the Festival.

Ferried in a fleet of 1975 black Chevrolet Impalas, driven as all cars seem to be in Cairo by handsome, wildly honking madmen, the international jury and symposium members moved from play to play, an imperial brigade, annoying throngs of men in flowing *galabiyyas* and women in the veil, babes in arms and burdens balanced gracefully on their heads. The central square of modern Cairo through which we careered each night is currently dominated by a huge poster for a film. A gigantic woman dressed in a black blood-spattered slip wields an axe. The film this poster advertises is based on an actual case of several years ago when a Cairene woman killed her husband, cut his body into pieces, and distributed them in plastic garbage bags around the city. Her act, though she is now in jail for life, set off a rash of eight or nine similarly desperate murders.

In a country where brothers can kill sisters on mere suspicion that they are no longer virgins and go scot free, and where at least 80 per cent (some say 97 per cent) of women have been genitally mutilated by clitoridectomy (though within the last ten years the practice is dying out in Cairo), the poster of the female axe-murderer lofted high above the streets in which many veiled and secular women are struggling for their rights and lives, spoke volumes. A major symposium on women's/feminist theatre would be impossible to hold in the United States right now, not because the situation of women and women's issues in the theatre has recently improved – the opposite is true – but because this decade's artistic fashion dictates 'gender' (read 'gay') and race issues are 'in', and women 'out'. Although, of course, until we face racism and sexism together, as twin world-wide pathologies, we will continue to be dominated by both.

Government involvement in the experimental theatre (or, in the US case, the utter lack of it) is a theme that emerged in greater complexity as the Festival entries were viewed. In the US – one of the birthplaces, along with Eastern Europe – of modern experimental theatre, the theatre is now censored economically, thus effectively ensuring that only the most commercial work exists both for international export and internal consumption. In contrast, Saudi Arabia, which has no indigenous theatre (since there is a prohibition against representation in strict Muslim tradition) created a work especially for the Cairo Festival in order to pretend to be part of the international arts community.

And since the Arab nations are admitted to the Festival without scrutiny by the pre-selection committee, the Saudi entry – laughable by most aesthetic standards, if it were not so ironic by standards of human rights – gains entry. Young men (no women allowed, of course) dressed in jump suits painted in a few bright colours cavort on stage for an hour looking like nothing so much as over-sized pre-schoolers. Their fabulist performance called The Lighthouse asks us to ponder why, though the one true way clearly exists (in the personification of the lighthouse), men are still so reluctant to follow the light. The only other piece as silly was provided by the Russians, an endless balletic faux-romance, featuring stuffed strawberries and grapes, antlers, and even leather halters and whips, provoking fury from the tired judges.

Egypt's official Festival entries were also fabulist. In the large opera house, a big dance piece,

Shady Abdel Salam's Desert, in which pharaohs, mummies, and harem dancers moved in front of a projection of the pyramids, was nothing more than high-kitsch travelogue. Another piece, more daring, was danced in hypnotizing unison by sixty young men in tee-shirts and jeans to Ravel's 'Bolero', while a large white scrotal sack descended slowly from the ceiling inside which writhed a human figure. This group-masturbatory effort climaxed with the music as the sack touched ground, virgin-birthing a young man for the curtain call.

The best Egyptian entries, and they were quite fine, existed outside the Festival competition. The El Warshaw company directed by Hassan El-Geretly, a half-Egyptian, half-Scot, refuses government funding altogether, so as to avoid the censor. They have been involved for many years in researching and reviving story-telling, stick dancing, and other indigenous performance techniques from the Arab world. Company members are a mix of traditional performers, both young and old, and trained actors.

In a tent at the back of the British Consulate we saw an open rehearsal of the Helaleyya Epic, the Arabic equivalent of the Iliad. While this work has not yet found a riveting dramatic shape, the magnificent faces, deep concentration, and mesmerizing rhythmic singing of the performers is powerful and intriguing. But the male posturing of the stick-dancing against the lascivious belly dancing of the women, though lively and engaging, made me impatient to see these time-worn stereotypes broken open and transformed.

A brief thirty-five minute work, called Hymn, which mixes ancient Arabic and African vocal, instrumental, and story-telling traditions with a unique, compelling, and modern ritual sound, is directed by Intisar Abdul Fattah. A chorus of men and women led by a female 'grandmother/priestess' relate the tale of a man from birth to death, while a woman and man dance the relationships in front. The male dancer plays 'the man', the woman dances 'his mother' and 'his wife', who is left alone to mourn his death. Again, the vocal work, astonishing and beautiful, underlined a romantic dance which was trite.

In medieval Islamic Cairo, in the beautiful Zenaib Khatoun Islamic house behind El Azhar mosque, the young, hardly trained, Rebellious Theatre performed A Journey, a wordless and completely free adaptation of Brecht's Seven Deadly Sins of the Petite Bourgeoisie by director Hany Ghanem. Kept out of Festival competition because of scanty male dress, this piece more than any other Egyptian work I saw addressed honestly and in pure, strong, raw theatrical imagery the dilemma of the male/female split and its relationship to poverty and war. Following experimental tradition from the 'sixties, the audience moved from space to space in the old house to witness seven discrete scenes. The sets were made from garbage, the ubiquitous plastic bags which litter the entire world, including the Khan El Khalili bazaar and the Sahara desert.

In *Birth*, a woman writhes in pain, delivering through a rusted oil barrel the new-born son, and continues to writhe until the after-birth appears, a rusted muffler of a car. In *Love*, a man sits rocking, mesmerized by the blond Barbie doll he holds in his hands, while a woman stands behind a silver image of a female bodice with black paper breasts, and masturbates, slowly turning a spoked rubber tire between her legs. In *Pain*, a dying man lies on the floor, a woman tries to do the work of the hovel in which they live and wails her grief. In *Bigotry*, hands are cut from men, who cry in pain, blood flows. In *Escape*, a man crawls and moans in a circle of wet sand, and the audience has literally to step over his bare body in order to escape.

Never during the entire piece do the men rise from the floor. They are permanently crouching, crawling, eternal little boys, done in by poverty, war, bigotry, and their own chauvinism. The women are interchangeable as mothers/wives, and endlessly enduring. It seemed to me an apt, strong, culturally specific, and therefore universal social critique.

A Lebanese entry, *Love Affair*, is the story told by a woman of her lover's suicide because of the pain of his involvement in the long civil war, the torture he suffered in prison, and the deaths of his comrades. The story seemed compelling (though there was no accurate translation for any of the language pieces) but the acting was forced, the actress pitched too high as if hysteria was her sole response to suffering.

The Tunisian dance theatre, *Without Nothing*, was a bold, sparse, angry, witty and, to me, important, moving, and beautiful series of scenes of street-life poverty. I saw what I need to see in theatre – into the inner life, the soul of misery revealed. A recurring violin solo and a single shaft of light in which an expressive dancer was repeatedly trapped; props, again, of city street garbage; and an ensemble working in close and intricate physical contact – all elements of a fierce aesthetic statement denouncing poverty. The fury of the dancers, their rage that such suffering exists, their disdain for the privileged who watch, reminded me of the poor of New York.

Dancers picked their noses, scratched their rears, spat masticated rolls at the audience, and one called an audience member a 'dirty European whore'. Here was none of the acceptance and serene Cairene submission, and for this reason, I suspect, the piece, which arguably was among the best in the Festival, did not fare well with all the judges.

The Greek entry, *Atrides*, was as sublime in its tragedy as the Tunisians were in their rage. Per-

formed outside, at the Giza pyramids, the Sphinx offering silent commentary, the juxtaposition of the monumental works of two great Mediterranean cultures was thrilling in itself. Like the *Atrides* of French director Ariane Mnouchkine, the Greek Spring Theatre began the cycle with Euripides' *Iphigenia in Aulis*, thus setting the context for Clytemnestra's husband-murder, but, unlike Mnouchkine, they stopped after *The Libation Bearers*, avoiding the patriarchal legal victory of *The Eumenides* and ending their trilogy with a tableau of brother and sister alone on stage, longing for one another across the great divide of revenge, raising again the issue of the sexes, and a deeper question of how we children of historical tragedy can become at last adults. Unlike Mnouchkine, the Greek company focused not on the spectacle of a leaping chorus, but on deep feeling. The six-woman chorus moved in simple, severe patterns, their voices rich with meaning.

One actress so physically slight that she seemed literally not to exist as a body, but as a fierce, raging spirit simply, played the daughters, Iphigenia, Cassandra, and Electra, and won the best actress award of the Festival. Tragedy is defined by the moment when we know ourselves as separate from our fates, and yet walk toward them, like Cassandra going knowingly to death. Tragically, we become ourselves most thoroughly the moment external fate strikes hard against the essence of the inner life, destroying comfort and the privilege we thought we had. The insignificance and magnitude of self and self-awareness becomes more tragic played against the austere lines of the Giza pyramids, and this Greek production made the tragic irony brilliantly clear.

A new Romanian play, *The Flood*, quite wonderfully acted if one likes pure emotion as I do, a comedy from Qatar critical of state bureaucracy, a Cypriot *Lysistrata* partly in drag, and a Bhuto-inspired meditative dance-theatre event from Australia provided other Festival high points.

The British entry, *70 Mill Lane*, by the Improbable Theatre, won the Festival, and an inventive, light, and ecologically aware piece from the Italian Laboratorio Teatro Settima came second. The jury voted a special citation to the Algerian entry, in the face of reports of a new slaughter of three hundred people, commending their bravery for making experimental theatre amidst such danger.

There was no theatrical entry from the Palestinians, none from Israel was offered or admitted, or from the US: yet the relation of these three peoples was uppermost in many minds. As the only North American who spoke in public, I felt it important to reveal myself not only as a Jew but a pacifist who stands against state-sponsored violence as well as terrorism, and as an artist whose work takes shape from these concerns.

The response to my talk brought me into contact with Arab and African female and male translators, journalists, artists, and observers. We stood in corridors, sat in lobbies or hotel rooms, drank tea, asked questions, interviewed each other. We spoke of peace and human rights, and of the condition of women. They said I was different from their idea of Americans; but so were they – bold, open, tolerant, gentle, some women wearing the veil, some wearing jeans or form-fitting dresses, each man and woman, individual and unique – different from any idea of 'the Arab'.

I interviewed a young half-German, half-Egyptian man who tried to make a film about Jews and Arabs living together, but has had his footage confiscated by the Egyptian censor. Yet, he chooses to live in Egypt because he found German racism intolerable. His German mother lives in Egypt, too.

A young translator is writing his Master's thesis on the works of three African-American women writers; he needs me to send him articles he cannot find in Egypt. A journalist who wears the veil interviewed me at length on assignment for the Egyptian Ministry of Culture quarterly magazine, and we became friends. She asked to read my play about genetic engineering and reproductive technologies. A Jordanian who teaches Shakespeare wants to read my play about Sappho but can't invite me to lecture at his university since I have revealed I'm Jewish. A Syrian woman tells me how, despite the lack of democracy, she struggles to find a form to reach directly to the hearts of people.

For the Arab, African, European, North and South American women playwrights and directors who spoke at the symposiums the problems are the same, though terribly relative; in each country there is not enough money, and scant respect for women artists. Dalia Basyouni from Egypt says there are only four women directors in the country, though one is head of the National Theatre. Karen Johnson from Britain laments funding cut-backs. Mariam Mayoumbila from Chad speaks wearily of the problem of lack of education for girls, who must resort to prostitution just to live.

And all of us women speak of the difficulty of getting women's plays produced. The effects of censorship appear in all shapes and sizes – political or economic, often both, and frequently emotional or self-censorship, the constant battle wearing one down. Despite the symposium topic, there is not one play in the Festival written or conceived by a woman. As usual at these events, we are allowed to talk to one another but not to do, in public, before an audience. The accepted male image of what might happen should a woman take action is enshrined on the film poster in downtown Cairo and, in Greek tragedy, as axe-wielding, vengeful Clytemnestra.

Women artists who create other, more complex, images of women, though present, do not have our work represented, and at the Cairo Festival we have to make do with *The Journey* and *Atrides*, both conceived and directed by men after original work by men, which, nevertheless, by challenging sexist stereotypes and images, also move world culture toward necessary change.

Peta Tait

Unstable Performative Elements

Physical Theatre's International Festival, Tollwood, Munich, June–July 1997.

TREAD WATER and conflate cultural spaces could have been the theme for the physical theatre and new circus programme at the tenth Tollwood Festival in Munich. On 6 July, at mid-festival, the unrelenting summer rain caused the French aerialist troupe, Les Arts Sauts, to cancel its outdoor evening show, threatened the music and other performance programmes, including the opening of Robert Wilson's *Persephone*, but provided the Argentine De La Guarda with the perfect backdrop for *Periodo Villa Villa*.

Spectators arrived wet at the Olympiahalle to find wet was also part of the spectatorial experience of *Periodo*. (Michael Jackson's concerts next door provided a synchronous association since De La Guarda members staged events at rock concerts and sports stadiums in the mid-1980s.) In *Periodo*, the most unique and imaginative show at Tollwood, directed by performers Diqui James and Pichon Baldinu, the group move bodies in the air as if they are crossing a terrorist action with a rave party. They claim: 'Our desire is complete rebellion.'

Periodo started with shadows moving across a beautiful low, green-blue (paper) ceiling a few feet above the 'submerged' audience, who were crowded together in a blacked-out space reminiscent of a dance party. The roof, pierced first by party decorations, was gradually ripped open by the weight of performing bodies swinging out on ropes just above the spectators' heads: a spectacle of bodies mid-air in fast, circular motion. Were they swimming or flying? As well as hand-operated pulleys, the group used motorized rigs (electric winches) which allowed the performers to move at speed and at height.

Sometimes they became remote figures vertically traversing a gigantic white screen. But mostly they worked close up, crawling among and over the audience. Suddenly an audience member would be lifted off the ground in a swooping raid as if the performers were pirates – the shipwrecked survivors of an earlier image when five bodies clung to, and hauled on, ropes in mid-air while the sea sprayed around them. The staging directly above the spectators, the wet, and the bodily contact made the experience of the show's concepts visceral, closer to a fun park ride than the safe theatrical voyeurism of watching distant athletic bodies. Wet: precarious, dangling bodies marking out danger zones. Wet: slippery, out of control.

Narrative beginnings in *Periodo* were quickly severed by wild action. The mood-evoking, original electronic and live music was all-pervasive, although the live instrumentation was only visible at the finale. But it was the four female dancers with their mini-skirted crotch display – together with one male dancer they comprise El Descueve – who were hypnotically compelling. The male performers in suits or disrobed, and working on mid-air apparatus, were less distinctive figures. But the familiarity of gender-defined street costumes was offset by these anarchic female bodies in action: the cruel ferociousness of their gaze, their seductive invitations and man-handling rebuttals.

Periodo is a major innovation in the physical theatre genre because the spectators' own bodily experiences of the show overlap in places with those of the performers: the separation between their sensory spaces is repeatedly breached. This sets up a risky phenomenology of spectatorship, for the spectators' reflexes are implicated in the unstable environment around performing bodies which are subverting even the spatial axis of the aerialist. But De La Guarda do not alienate their spectators, and instead like aerialists the group enchant, dazzle, exhilarate, and thrill; they celebrate with us.

By comparison with the performance by the North American Second Hand Dance Company, the highly skilled De La Guarda, working across forms and reflecting a continuum in the practice of suspending dancers on harnesses begun in the early 1970s, led me to ask whose outdated notion of a movement text were the untrained, three-man company satirizing? Continuing the theme of wet, *Drift*, by the Dutch Vis à Vis, which I did not see, also used floating and submerged bodies.

The Danish Acid Cirque's *Inferno* was in a circular space ringed by aquariums full of water, but, due to prohibitions, without their performing eels. Despite a funereal aesthetic and a good level of individual skills ranging from motorbike manoeuvring to slackwire, this show remained conventional circus, a series of acts with some gender identity fusion. The male jugglers put on frocks while the Swedish cradle (trapeze) act of Angela Hinas and Sara Sandquist conveyed images of defiantly muscular, strong women.

On 7 July the rain held off long enough for a last performance by Les Arts Sauts on their freestanding rig, which rises into place at the beginning of the show like a ship being launched. It was wet, windy, and dangerous, and unavoidably the fliers missed some of their more difficult somersaults. In this classical aerial act, white illuminated bodies worked against a night sky without narratives, props, or, despite the French legacy of the famous cross-dressing Babette, signs of the queer and gender-defiant bodies evident in much new circus from other countries.

Reinhard Bischel, who was promoter-producer of the Tollwood physical theatre programme, had brought over two groups from Australia, where physical theatre is very prominent. In *All of Me,* written by Mary Morris and directed by Nigel Jamieson, Legs on the Wall explore the tear-filled emotional spaces of a heterosexual relationship break-up and its impact on two children. The wide-eyed, thirty-something Kathryn Neische was completely child-like in her dives from up high. Surprisingly, bodies in continual acrobatic movement with few words could yet convey emotions. While the scenario is commonplace, the show's physical theatre form offers the insight that a family exists in continuous physical contact so that its break-up is one of bodily separation. In contrast, Australia's grunge-style Acrobat, working on a free-standing rig, disrupted the cultural space of circus as wholesome family entertainment in pursuit of Archaos sensibilities and furthering its men-in-frocks aesthetic with Simon Mitchell's queer drag act on a web (single rope).

Is physical theatre's recent fascination with water because its properties are unstable like air – and gender and sexual identity – and create spaces still to be conquered in performance? Or are these shows evidence of watery eruptions from the cultural unconscious at the end of the millennium? I am reminded of several other recent performance experiments with space and water in Australia – an island country keenly aware of how water generates spatial separations in cultural geographies. Interestingly, De La Guarda, which presented the most radical conflation of performance forms and spaces at Tollwood, comes from Argentina, another southern hemisphere country probably having to confront the loss of its cultural illusions of unrestricted vastness.

NTQ Book Reviews

edited by Maggie Gale

Theatre History to 1900

Stephen Orgel
**Impersonations: the Performance
of Gender in Shakespeare 's England**
Cambridge University Press, 1996. £10.95.
ISBN 0-521-56842-0.

Orgel begins with the question of why the English renaissance stage was so singularly, and 'unnecessarily', committed to having boys perform the parts of women. This leads into an account of how, in the matter of Renaissance gender, things were not as simple as modern criticism makes out. Thus the notion that all women were alike victimized by all men – a situation brought about by that favourite ogre of student essays, 'the' patriarchy – has to be expanded in order to allow for the fact of women apprentices, the differential empowerment of class, male effeminacy alongside female 'masculinity', and the erotic fix on boys alongside that on women.

All this is very clearly, if slightly repetitively, written, which makes the book user-friendly in an academic field which has more than its fair share of ornamental obscurities. Orgel's strength is in the sharp local perception – the scholarly insistence, for example, that despite the fantasies of critics and directors the text of *Edward II* does not call for an on-stage poker. Such rigour is a useful corrective to critical orthodoxies which abjure the unfashionably empirical.

But Orgel's rigour tends to limit itself to verbal and painted texts: that word 'performance' in his title has much more to do with trendy concepts of gender than with the business of working on a stage. Which is a problem, for a more theatrically-aware analysis might be drawn to inquire what sort of thing the boy's body was on the Renaissance stage. This should lead, pretty crucially, to a definition of what a Renaissance 'boy' might be. But no: while womanhood may be 'performed', boys will be boys, naturally.

SIMON SHEPHERD

Meg Twycross, ed.
Festive Drama
Woodbridge: Brewer, 1996. £35.00.
ISBN 0-859-91496-8.

Radical theatre practitioners keep returning to explore the theatre/performance boundary. I write this review at the time of the 1997 LIFT festival, which includes under the heading of 'theatre' processions around a dockland installation, circus, fireworks, and losing oneself in the Roundhouse basement. In the context of such work, it is interesting to cast back to the medieval world where theatre did not exist as a discrete entity. There was no classical/renaissance assumption that 'theatre' is based on imitation, thus requiring an imitator and a passive viewer of the imitation.

Later theatre historians have carved out arbitrarily a selection of medieval practices that can conveniently be slotted into a continuous history of 'theatre'. Meg Twycross's anthology is a useful corrective to this renaissance perspective, documenting a series of festive practices that stand in a liminal area between theatre and cultural performance.

The essays derive from a colloquium organized by the International Society for the Study of Medieval Theatre in 1989. There is the normal problem of uneven quality that one expects in such a collection. The spread is international, with Spain and the Netherlands enjoying a high profile. The richest studies are those of English material, reflecting the huge impact of the Records of Early English Drama (REED) project, which has made a different level of investigation possible. The best work in medieval drama is being conducted on a local level, as researchers demonstrate the interface between paratheatrical practices, small town politics, and the desire of communities and communities within communities to assert a distinctive and exclusive group identity.

The world that emerges from this book is one of ongoing social conflict rather than organic wholeness, diversity rather than homogeneity under the rule of Rome. Attempts to theorize this material seem to have produced few advances in the last twenty or thirty years. Totalizing theories (Frazer, Victor Turner, Bakhtin, vulgar structuralism) seem to crumble when the diversity of local practices is placed under the microscope. Taking the overview is increasingly difficult.

A comparative European perspective has undoubtedly proved helpful to many working on English material, and I imagine that the *ésprit communautaire* has reciprocal benefits. For those seeking to sample the range of medieval festive fare, across Europe and across the calendar, *Festive Drama* is to be recommended. Those seeking an updated and succinct overview of what medieval drama was might be better advised to wait patiently for at least another twenty years.

DAVID WILES

Harry G. Carlson
Out of Inferno:
Strindberg's Reawakening as an Artist
University of Washington Press, 1996.
ISBN 0-295-97564-4.

Between 1892 and 1898 the normally prolific Strindberg wrote no plays. Indeed, during these years when he devoted himself primarily to scientific speculation, alchemy, and painting, and also underwent the spiritual and mental crisis recounted in the autobiographical fiction *Inferno* (1897), he produced virtually no literature of any kind. What renders these years so fascinating from a theatrical point of view is that when Strindberg eventually returned to drama with the first part of *To Damascus*, he emerged with a new kind of play, one that seemingly represented a radical departure from the masterpieces of the 1880s, *The Father, Miss Julie*, and *Creditors*.

Precisely how he achieved this personal renewal in which he also effected the transition from naturalism to modernism in the theatre is the subject of Harry Carlson's important book. While he concentrates on Strindberg's prose writings and refers only occasionally to the plays, Carlson does here offer the most thoroughgoing study of the artistic aspects of this crucial period in the making of modern drama. He discriminates with great skill among the various impulses to which Strindberg responded in *fin-de-siècle* Berlin and Paris, and highlights the importance for his new way of seeing of Paul Gauguin and Edvard Munch.

For while, as Carlson demonstrates, he responds acutely to the orientalism, occultism, and medievalism of the period, it is his painting that now enabled Strindberg to experiment with new methods of representation and ultimately to rehabilitate his confidence in the role of the imagination – on which his later and most crucial contribution to modern drama depends. These years were the crucible in which the dramaturgy of *To Damascus*, *A Dream Play*, and *The Ghost Sonata* were forged, and thanks to Carlson we are now very much better able to appreciate this. This is a fascinating book and a major contribution to our knowledge of the period.

MICHAEL ROBINSON

John Stokes
Oscar Wilde: Myths, Miracles, and Imitations
Cambridge: Cambridge University Press, 1996.
ISBN 0-521-47537-6.

Instead of the unitary, radical, and subversive Wilde who emerges from a great deal of recent criticism, we encounter here not one but many Wildes – as memorialized in the diary of a friend, as a character on stage and in film, as a reader of the Romantic poets, as a tourist in Dieppe, as a character in recent stagings of his own plays. What joins these somewhat diffuse concerns for Stokes is the idea of re-enactment, his conviction that Wilde is not one but many, reproducible into many different images.

The first chapter, for example, identifies 'an oral Wilde, who is at least as well known as the written Wilde'. The focus here is on a story called *The Magic Ball*, told by Wilde on several occasions and given varied expression in print by friends of Wilde, including Frank Harris and Louis Latourrette. The 'magic ball' belongs to a savant or illusionist who claims to be able to make it move on command, spontaneously. It is a claim which the events of the story at least partly corroborate, even though the printed versions involve a child or dwarf concealed inside the 'great ball' to make sure it responds on command.

Calling upon histories of the circus to find a context for Wilde's story of the magic ball, Stokes fleshes out the story of a Romanian contortionist called LaRoche, who in the 1890s toured Europe with an act which bore curious resemblances to Wilde's oral story and was treated in a novel of the 1950s called *The Magic Ball*. This, writes Stokes, is 'the kind of coincidence that makes history real . . . a material miracle with a humane message'.

As an imaginative, at times lyrical analysis of a non-existent work by Wilde, this essay on the magic ball is at once impressive and unique. But in this book of 'Wilde's many different images' we do not have much opportunity to reflect before moving on to the next topic, another relatively unexplored region of Wilde's life or work and the context in which it was situated. In the ensuing chapter Stokes introduces the anonymous writer 'I. Playfair', author of an obscure pamphlet defending Wilde after his conviction, *Some Gentle Criticisms of British Justice*.

'Playfair' is identified as James H. Wilson, an enthusiast of Lord Alfred Douglas and a poet in his own right. His various compositions and unsuccessful attempts to place his pro-Wilde pamphlet in *Reynolds' Newspaper* are described by Stokes to show the marginal Wilson as symbolically central, standing for a newly developing constituency of moral protesters in the 1890s. The Oscar Wilde reproduced thereby is a humanitarian one, 'the enemy of official hypocrisy'. But what is more fascinating than this version of Wilde is Stokes's revelation of the otherwise unknown Playfair, or James Wilson, giving life to an obscure figure by exploring for the first time the role he played in the events of Oscar Wilde's life.

The same point could be made about Stokes's excellent chapter on the nearly forgotten George Ives, poet, humanitarian, and advocate of rights for homosexuals. Ives, a friend of Wilde in the 1890s, left besides his poetry a massive amount of writing and memorabilia in the form of scrap-books, manuscripts, and a 122-volume diary – nearly all unpublished, and much of it, including the huge diary, now housed in the Humanities Research Center at the University of Texas.

Stokes provides what is apparently the first real interpretation of these materials, especially the diary, and focuses of course on their relation, and their author's, to Wilde. For example, Stokes points out that Wilde assigned the address of Ives's homosexual menage in Piccadilly to the chambers occupied by a character in an early version of *The Importance of Being Earnest*. Beginning in 1892, Wilde and Lord Alfred Douglas were frequently in the company of Ives, often entertained in his rooms along with other homosexual guests. Ives recalls Wilde passionately kissing him on one occasion, and on another expresses guilt over an apparent sexual encounter with Douglas.

But Ives, a self-described 'evolutionary anarchist', was deeply committed to social reform and lamented in his diary that Wilde was not – that he 'had not the gift of responsibility, he could not estimate consequence, he was all Art, and all Emotion, and I looked up to him as to a super-man (and do still), while utterly disagreeing with his written philosophy, and even with his life, on many sides'. When Wilde died, however, Ives wrote of him in his diary as a 'victim and martyr,' and of his death as 'the greatest tragedy of the whole nineteenth century'.

Other versions of Wilde occupy other chapters, but none succeeds so brilliantly as the chapter on Ives. Wilde seems a peripheral figure in 'Romantic Reincarnations', an essay on Victorian interpretations of the Romantic poets, and again in a chapter on the 'art of deformation' in Aubrey Beardsley and Alfred Jarry. An interesting essay concerns itself with *fin-de-siècle* holidays in Dieppe – 'another world', as one novelist of the time had called it, leisurely and fantastic, where consumerist London could be put out of mind. A final chapter examines recent productions of Wilde's plays by Philip Prowse, Peter Hall, and others, finding in general a lavish deployment of costume and design aimed at reproducing by visual means Wilde's extravagance of language.

Stokes's analysis is fascinating, in part because of its attention to what reviewers have said about these Wildean revivals. Rarely did they catch a glimpse of the radical Wilde materialized in much recent criticism of Wilde, instead finding that, in these plays, 'melodrama and its sentimentality were written with serious intent, as if Wilde genuinely believed in the importance of being earnest'. The reactions of these critics often remind me of the disappointed sighs of Wilde's friend and self-professed radical George Ives, confessing to his diary when writing of Wilde: 'On many points I cannot defend him.'

While adding to our knowledge of the context of Oscar Wilde, John Stokes provides further evidence of the variousness and complexity of Wilde himself. *Oscar Wilde: Myths, Miracles, and Imitations* will complicate matters for those who would like to confine Wilde within the scope of a singleminded personality or politics.

KERRY POWELL

Twentieth-Century Theatre

Colin Counsell
Signs of Performance: an Introduction to Twentieth-Century Theatre
London: Routledge, 1996. £ 10.99 (pbk).
ISBN 0-415-10643-5.

Signs of Performance joins a number of other recent offerings from Routledge which aim to corner the undergraduate market. Counsell sets himself a rather awesome task here: 'to examine the theatre of the West in the twentieth century and to bring to bear upon it the analytical perspectives that have been developed in recent years and which are now central to the work in other disciplines'.

The introduction contextualizes the book's emphasis on 'Dead White Bourgeois Males' who have historically dominated theatre practice. The author aims to challenge 'orthodoxy' from a position which 'view(s) the existing canon critically', rather than 'draw into the centre of the enquiry practitioners who have been marginalized'. In taking the reader from Stanislavski's 'System' to 'Performance Art and Postmodernism' *via* individual chapters on Strasberg, Brecht, Beckett, Brook, and Robert Wilson, the author's achievements lie equally between providing a theoretical framework for the discussion of each practitioner, and outlining this in a language which makes the subject accessible to the 'new' reader.

However, the absence of chapters on a number of key figures from within the 'existing canon' begs certain questions. One would presume that considerations of the work of Meyerhold, Artaud, and Grotowski would lend themselves usefully to this study. We are also told in the marketing blurb that the book 'assumes no previous knowledge of the subject or of the theories'. It may however somewhat ironically 'signify' to the unsuspecting undergraduate an inherent appropriateness in the unification of subject and theory. *Signs of Performance* – in some ways to be commended – none the less raises far more questions than it answers, not only regarding the introductory text, but by implication the current academic status of theatre studies, and divisions of approach within the teaching of the discipline at undergraduate level.

JOHN DEENEY

Arthur Holmberg
Directors in Perspective:
the Theatre of Robert Wilson
Cambridge University Press, 1996. £37.50.
ISBN 0-521-36492-2.

Holmberg's book may be seen as the third volume of a Wilson trilogy, following Stefan Brecht's *The Theatre of Visions* (1978) and Shyer's *Robert Wilson and His Collaborators* (1989). Brecht's is a detailed study of Wilson's early work from the loft pieces in the 1960s to *I Was Sitting on My Patio* (1977). Shyer focuses on the tremendous collaborative energy required for Wilson to work, particularly after *Einstein on the Beach* (1976), when the whole process becomes highly professionalized and international. Holmberg's update to the 1990s includes Wilson's work with classics (for example, *King Lear* and *Danton's Death*) and grand opera (*Parzival*, *The Magic Flute*, *Lohengrin*, and *Madame Butterfly* in 1993, the last cited by Holmberg, although Wilson has continued with opera since then in his inimitable way).

Holmberg's special achievement lies in his acute attention not only to the aesthetic components of Wilson's work, but also to its aesthetic principles. He takes *A Letter for Queen Victoria* (1974) as a crossroads case, after which Wilson's 'strategies' for interrogating language (Holmberg collects ten, among them the disjunction and discontinuity of words) begin to lead away from pure semiotics towards semantic meaning.

This very pertinent distinction allows Holmberg to chart significant shifts in Wilson's *oeuvre* as well as to explain how Wilson, undoubtedly a gigantic innovator, appropriates classics to his elusive, allusive, and associative style. Holmberg illustrates many observations with commentaries from Wilson, with whom he has had privileged contact. The book is organized according to clusters of ideas which, with what feels like the help of a good editor, pulls together the prodigious amount of material Wilson has generated. Above all, it shows anyone who wishes to discover or rediscover Wilson just how marvellous he really is.

MARIA SHEVTSOVA

Geraldine Cousin
Women in Dramatic Place and Time
London: Routledge, 1996. £12.99 (pbk).
ISBN 0-415-06734-0.

The prologue to Geraldine Cousin's book uses Ibsen's Nora as a prototype for the characters who constitute her subject-matter. Cousin's self-styled journey beyond the doll's house' explores, in a largely celebratory fashion, the work of selected late twentieth-century plays by women dramatists and the 'interconnections' between the various female characters who feature in the discussion.

The book, Cousin states, is concerned with 'female characters' quests for clear and distinctive voices with which to tell their stories to date, and determine their future narratives, and with their attempts to leave, or alternatively to refashion, the environments in which they find themselves'. The six chapters certainly cover a lot of ground: the discussion ranges from the treatment of landscape and environment to female quest narratives and reworkings of myth, history, and auto/biography. Many of the plays included in Cousin's commentary will feature on undergraduate feminist theatre courses, but a number will not.

One of the problems with this kind of work, which features texts that are not readily available, is that the author is compelled to supply some form of synopsis. Given the vast terrain that Cousin navigates, there isn't space for much more than plot recapitulation and limited character study. There are six chapters, a prologue, and a 'retrospective', which in itself reduces the scope for analysis. Moreover, the coherence of the book depends on the 'interconnections' which Cousin seeks to establish. The objective may be to establish a different kind of non-linear structure, but the result is a book seemingly organized on a principle of association. Cousin describes this book as a 'journey'; as a passenger, I found the route at times circuitous and the connnections somewhat arbitrary.

NICOLA SHAUGHNESSY

Michael Billington,
The Life and Work of Harold Pinter
London: Faber and Faber, 1996. £20.00.
ISBN 0-571-l7l03-6.

Should critics go backstage? The risk these days is not so much bribery (what Victorians called the 'chicken and champagne' brand of reviewing) so much as intellectual persuasion, the heavy implication that the critic may have underestimated the difficulties, obscured the intention, that without some special information they will get things wrong, always be outsiders. There is something almost Faustian about the temptation to know more than is permitted an ordinary theatregoer, with the attendant threat that in gaining knowledge the critic may forego freedom.

It's a risk that Michael Billington, normally our most responsible and most intellectually confident critic, here seems prepared to take. Invited into Pinter's house, offered intimate confidences, even his prose takes on a disturbingly cowed air. At times (as in his analysis of *The Homecoming*, for example) he recants his own earlier judgement. His overall thesis, that Pinter's plays derive from personal experience, is entirely persuasive yet generally validated by Pinter's own testimony. Even when others give evidence, they are respectful. The impression, inevitably, is that we are being told what Pinter is prepared for us to hear.

The information is, it's true, hard to resist: not only the revelations about his lovers (not all of whom are named – reasonably enough), which are used to defend his portrayal of women on the grounds that independence is compatible with erotic appeal, but the tales of his days as a lad around Hackney and, subsequently, of his forays around the country as a jobbing actor. Remarkably, Pinter is a playwright of journeys, most of them short, usually within London, and (with the famous exception of a trip to Sidcup and the trials of Bolsover Street) quite easily executed.

London is familiar but boundless, zoned but permeable, whose inhabitants speak Pinterese – a lexical hybrid that can express, sometimes within a single sentence, cruelty, pretension, pedantry, and yearning. Stuck in single rooms they may be; verbally and topographically, like Pinter himself, who has gone from Hackney to Regent's Park to Holland Park, they are usually on the move.

As an actor, Pinter was obliged to perform in the rep standbys of the day, thrillers like Agatha Christie's *Murder at the Vicarage* or, rather better, Patrick Hamilton's *Rope*. Writing his own plays, he kept the tension, dumped or muddied the motivation. Unexplained interrogation became the classic Pinter mode. Billington, following in the steps of his subject, wants to claim that this lifelong preoccupation with the manipulation of power is enough to make him 'political', but that stretches the word too far.

The evidence of the plays, as of certain aspects of the life, suggest that Pinter is an instinctive humanitarian who portrays the irrationality of injustice without proposing some equally vulnerable ideological answer. This principle of opposition underlay his decision to be a Conscientious Objector in 1949 as much as it did his hostility to American imperialism in the 1980s: and, however courageous, it suggests a man whose moral anger is at one with intellectual caution.

Sometimes the parallels between the life and the work seem so consistent that it's a wonder we didn't see them before. Or perhaps some did, but, unlike Billington, felt that permitted disclosures, however fascinating, would fail to explain the powerfully theatrical evasions of the plays. Unless Pinter chooses to write an autobiography, Billington's book will not be duplicated: it may yet be expanded.

JOHN STOKES

Performance, Theory, General Studies

Marvin Carlson
Performance: a Critical Introduction
London; New York: Routledge, 1996. £9.99.
ISBN 0-415-13703-9.

This is vintage Carlson – erudite, concise, precise, and engaging. The book also shows to advantage Carlson's gift for stopping at significant landmarks in an overview to reflect upon their particular traits. It is a cartography of notions of performance as used in contemporary studies, whether in theatre, latter-day performance, or cultural studies. The ubiquity of the term comes from its rather heterogeneous sources, which Carlson properly situates in the anthropological work of Bateson, van Gennep, Turner, and Geertz, among others, and, inevitably, in the sociological play-roles-and-games theorists such as Huizinga, Caillois, and Goffman. Richard Schechner's important role in putting a lot of this together, and diffusing and publicizing it, is also warmly acknowledged.

All this makes the book very accessible to all kinds of students, and it will deservedly become a textbook for introductory courses. Like all such introductions, however, it runs the risk of trivializing material that requires more serious handling, such as occurs in the pages on sociological approaches to the problems and the practices of performance. Carlson's view of sociology, as also of sociological perspectives on performance and theatre studies, is terribly out of date, assuming that these can be reduced to matters of causality, positivism, or behaviourism. Yet sociology, not least in relation to performance and theatre, has come a long way from its facts and figures, case study, and direct mirror-of-life mentality, particularly as expounded in the United States in the 1950s and 1960s; and it has moved on in the US, as well. A similarly, rather too localized view is given of performance and the postmodern.

Still, this tendency to focus on his own socio-cultural terrain is necessary when it comes to situating the multiple *practices* that gave rise to concepts of performance in 'historical context'. Here Carlson covers a good deal of ground, taking the famous Black Mountain College manifestations (Cage, Cunningham, Tudor, *et al.*) and appropriately linking them back to the great pioneers of modern dance in the 1930s (Ruth St Denis, Ted Shawn, Graham, Humphrey, Wiedman), as well as forwards to such great performance artists as Laurie Anderson, Meredith Monk, and Robert Wilson.

The ins and outs of this performancescape include what for Carlson appear to be the main *problématiques* from the 1970s through the 1990s – women's performance, sex and gender identity, and what he calls 'resistant performance'. Much of it is too cursory – the problem, again, of the overview genre – and talks more about what academics say than performers do. But it would be carping to dwell on the insufficiencies of the genre when Carlson's shot of the horizon is admirable, coming, as it does, from a scholar who has contributed so much, and so generously, to our field.

MARIA SHEVSTOVA

Carl Miller
Stages of Desire: Gay Theatre's Hidden History
London; New York: Cassell, 1996.
ISBN 0-304-32815-4.

The increasing presence of gay and lesbian studies – within both theatre studies and cultural studies – has engendered an important body of research over recent years. However, Carl Miller's *Stages of Desire* possibly represents one of the most important contributions to this growing canon. Whilst much of the work in the field has hitherto been dominated by cultural theory, particularly the early influences of feminism, and latterly queer theory, Miller takes a refreshingly apposite approach.

Beginning with early English drama, and ending his analysis in the nineteenth century – making occasional contemporary parallel references *en route* – Miller provides us with some 250 pages of gay and lesbian 'hidden' theatre history, presenting the reader with new readings of both established and obscured texts. Additionally, the 'offstage' material of historical and theatrical records is employed to consider, for example, the 'Arse Play' in early English comedy, sodomy in Shakespeare, and 'out of the closet drama' from Restoration women playwrights.

Discerning critics may vilify *Stages in Desire* for Miller's emphasis on 'my own interests and perspectives', the sometimes irreverent style, and the conclusion that there 'is no lesbian and gay theatre. There is just theatre.' Nevertheless, the writer has considered the challenges of 'historical intercourse' when undertaking such a subject, and there is a wealth of valuable research here. *Stages in Desire*, along with the other titles in the Cassell sexual politics series, is not only concerned with the academic market: Miller works

primarily as a playwright and theatre director, and this experience reveals itself in his incisive dramaturgical exploration of the texts chosen. In offering genuinely new research, and in pointing to the importance of further historical research in the field of gay and lesbian theatre, Miller's book is a valuable and timely contribution.

JOHN DEENEY

Bonnie Marranca
Ecologies of Theatre
USA: Johns Hopkins University Press,
PAJ Books, 1996. £13.00 (pbk).
ISBN 0-801-85273-0.

This is an eclectic collection of Bonnie Marranca's essays, reviews, discussions, and talks subtitled 'Essays at the Century Turning'. She draws on a wide range of practitioners and practices, but her predominant frame is post-war American performance and culture with constant reference to Gertrude Stein, 'the Mother of the avant garde', and Robert Wilson's 'theatre of images'. Among others she writes on Rachel Rosenthal, Maria Irene Fornes, John Cage, Spalding Gray, Meredith Monk, and Heiner Müller.

The American emphasis may make several essays inaccessible to the European reader – and none more so than a discussion entitled 'The Controversial 1985-1986 Theater Season'. The book excites when evaluating European movements, both cultural and political, from her objective geographical position in New York, that most 'European' of melting-pots. Marranca's writing is always politically sensitive and this dates the earlier pieces: yet in the next moment she fascinates with discussions of biology, chaos theory, or plate tectonics, carrying forward the writings of Herbert Blau (to whom the book is dedicated).

Her depth of analysis and all-encompassing knowledge are fired by her vision and concern for the future of performance. With this further step towards defining an 'ecology of theatre' she offers an enlightening perspective on nature as inspiration, as a performative element, and as a compositional framing device. In her discussions of place, space, and cultural identity, she reveals not only her passion for gardening but (more significantly at the turn of the century) that perhaps it is 'not so difficult to move from a theatre to a landscape'.

PAUL ALLAIN